SPAM AND INTERNET PRIVACY

INTERNET PRIVACY

Novinka Books
New York

SPAM AND INTERNET PRIVACY

B.G. KUTAIS
EDITOR

Novinka Books
New York

PREFACE

The issues covered in this book cannot be called hot issues but instead must be called 'boiling' issues. Who, except the senders of this dangerous and ever-more sophisticated material, is not attacked everyday? What laws protect us if any? What is being done about it if anything? This new book presents the latest progress on these issues which rate extremely high on everyone's list of concerns.

In: Spam and Internet Privacy
Editor: B.G. Kutais, pp. 1-29 ISBN: 978-1-59454-577-1
© 2007 Nova Science Publishers, Inc.

Chapter 1

"SPAM": AN OVERVIEW OF ISSUES CONCERNING COMMERCIAL ELECTRONIC MAIL[*]

Marcia S. Smith

SUMMARY

Spam, also called unsolicited commercial email (UCE) or "junk email," aggravates many computer users. Not only can spam be a nuisance, but its cost may be passed on to consumers through higher charges from Internet service providers who must upgrade their systems to handle the traffic. Also, some spam involves fraud, or includes adult-oriented material that offends recipients or that parents want to protect their children from seeing. Proponents of UCE insist it is a legitimate marketing technique that is protected by the First Amendment, and that some consumers want to receive such solicitations.

On December 16, 2003, President Bush signed into law the Controlling the Assault of Non-Solicited Pornography and Marketing (CAN-SPAM) Act, P.L. 108-187. It went into effect on January 1, 2004. The CAN-SPAM Act does not ban UCE. Rather, it allows marketers to send commercial email as long as it conforms with the law, such as including a legitimate opportunity for consumers to "opt-out" of receiving future commercial

---

[*] Excerpted from CRS Report RL31953, Updated September 16, 2004

emails from that sender. It preempts state laws that specifically address spam, but not state laws that are not specific to email, such as trespass, contract, or tort law, or other state laws to the extent they relate to fraud or computer crime. It does not require a centralized "Do Not Email" registry to be created by the Federal Trade Commission (FTC), similar to the National Do Not Call registry for telemarketing. The law requires only that the FTC develop a plan and timetable for establishing such a registry, and to inform Congress of any concerns it has with regard to establishing it. The FTC submitted a report to Congress on June 15, 2004, concluding that a Do Not Email registry at this time would not reduce spam, and might increase it.

The extent to which the law reduces "spam" overall may be debated if for no other reason than there are various definitions of that term. Proponents of the law argue that consumers are most irritated by *fraudulent* email, and that the law should reduce the volume of such email because of the civil and criminal penalties included therein. Opponents counter that consumers object to *unsolicited* commercial email, and since the law legitimizes commercial email (as long as it conforms with the law's provisions), consumers actually may receive more, not fewer, UCE messages. Thus, whether or not "spam" is reduced depends in part on whether it is defined as only fraudulent commercial email, or all unsolicited commercial email.

Many observers caution that consumers should not expect any law to solve the spam problem — that consumer education and technological advancements also are needed. The Internet industry is working on technological solutions, such as creating an authentication standard to reduce "spoofing," where spammers use false addresses in the "from" line to avoid spam filters and deceive recipients into opening the message. The FTC and Consumers Union are among the groups offering consumer education tips.

Spam on wireless devices such as cell phones is a growing concern, and is addressed CRS Report RL31636. This report will be updated.

OVERVIEW

One aspect of increased use of the Internet for electronic mail (e-mail) has been the advent of unsolicited advertising, also called "unsolicited commercial e-mail" (UCE), "unsolicited bulk e-mail," "junk e-mail, "or "spam."[1] (**This report does not address junk mail or junk fax.** See CRS Report RS32177 or CRS Report RS21647, respectively, for information on those topics.)

Complaints focus on the fact that some spam contains, or has links to, pornography, that much of it is fraudulent, and the volume of spam is steadily increasing. In April 2003, the Federal Trade Commission (FTC) reported that of a random survey of 1,000 pieces of spam, 18% concerned "adult" offers (pornography, dating services, etc.) and 66% contained indications of falsity in "from" lines, "subject" lines, or message text.[2] According to Brightmail [http://www.brightmail.com], a company that sells anti-spam software, the volume of spam as a percentage of all Internet e-mail rose from 8% in January 2001 to 65% in July 2004.

Opponents of junk e-mail argue that not only is it annoying and an invasion of privacy (see CRS Report RL31408 for more on Internet privacy), but that its cost is borne by recipients and Internet Service Providers (ISPs), not the marketers. Consumers reportedly are charged higher fees by ISPs that must invest resources to upgrade equipment to manage the high volume of e-mail, deal with customer complaints, and mount legal challenges to junk e-mailers. Businesses may incur costs due to lost productivity, or investing in upgraded equipment or anti-spam software. The Ferris Research Group [http://www.ferris.com], which offers consulting services on managing spam, estimated in 2003 that spam cost U.S. organizations over $10 billion.

Proponents of UCE argue that it is a valid method of advertising, and is protected by the First Amendment. The Direct Marketing Association (DMA) released figures in May 2003 showing that commercial e-mail generates more than $7.1 billion in annual sales and $1.5 billion in potential savings to American consumers.[3] In a joint open letter to Congress published in *Roll Call* on November 13, 2003, three marketing groups — DMA, the American Association of Advertising Agencies, and the Association of National Advertisers — asserted that "12% of the $138 billion Internet commerce marketplace is driven by legitimate commercial e-mail. This translates into a minimum of $17.5 billion spent in response to commercial e-mails in 2003 for bedrock goods and services such as travel, hotels, entertainment, books, and clothing."[4] A March 2004 study by the Pew Internet & American Life Project found that 5% of e-mail users said they had ordered a product or service based on an unsolicited e-mail, which "translates into more than six million people."[5]

DMA argued for several years that instead of banning UCE, individuals should be given the opportunity to "opt-out" by notifying the sender that they want to be removed from the mailing list. (The concepts of opt-out and opt-in are discussed below.) Hoping to demonstrate that self regulation could work, in January 2000, the DMA launched the E-mail Preference Service where consumers who wish to opt-out can register themselves at a DMA website [http://www.dmaconsumers .org/emps.html]. DMA members sending UCE must check their lists of recipients and delete those who have opted out. Critics argued that most spam does not come from DMA members, so the plan was insufficient, and on October 20, 2002, the DMA agreed. Concerned that the volume of unwanted and fraudulent spam is undermining the use of e-mail as a marketing tool, the DMA announced that it would pursue legislation to battle the rising volume of spam.

Controlling spam is complicated by the fact that some of it originates outside the United States and thus is not subject to U.S. laws or regulations. Spam is a global problem, and a 2001 study by the European Commission concluded that Internet subscribers globally pay 10 billion Euros a year in connection costs to download spam [http://europa.eu.int/comm/ internal_market/privacy/studies/spam_en.htm]. Some European officials complain that the United States is the source of most spam, and the U.S. decision to adopt an opt-out approach in the CAN-SPAM Act (discussed below) was not helpful.[6] In an August 2004 report, a British anti-spam and anti-virus software developing company, Sophos, listed the United States as the largest spam producing country, exporting 42.5% of spam (South Korea was second, at 15.4%).[7] That figure is a drop from 56% that Sophos reported for the United States in February 2004.[8] Tracing the origin of any particular piece of spam can be difficult because some spammers route their messages through other computers (discussed below) that may be located anywhere on the globe.

WHAT IS SPAM?

One challenge in debating the issue of spam is defining it.[9] To some, it is any commercial e-mail to which the recipient did not "opt-in" by giving prior *affirmative consent* to receiving it. To others, it is commercial e-mail to which *affirmative* or *implied consent* was not given, where implied consent can be defined in various ways (such as whether there is a pre-existing business relationship). Still others view spam as "unwanted" commercial e-mail. Whether or not a particular e-mail is unwanted, of course, varies per recipient. Since senders of UCE do find buyers for some of their products, it can be argued that at least some UCE is reaching interested consumers, and therefore is wanted, and thus is not spam. Consequently, some argue that marketers should be able to send commercial e-mail messages as long as they allow each recipient an opportunity to indicate that future such e-mails are not desired (called "opt-out"). Another group considers spam to be only fraudulent commercial e-mail, and believe that commercial e-mail messages from "legitimate" senders should be permitted. The DMA, for example, considers spam to be only fraudulent UCE.

The differences in defining spam add to the complexity of devising legislative or regulatory remedies for it. Some of the bills introduced in the 108th Congress took the approach of defining commercial e-mail, and permitting such e-mail to be sent to recipients as long as it conformed with certain requirements. Other bills defined *unsolicited* commercial e-mail and prohibited it from being sent unless it met certain requirements. The final law, the CAN-SPAM Act (see below), took the former approach, defining and allowing marketers to send such e-mail as long as they abide by the terms of the law, such as ensuring that the e-mail does not have fraudulent header information or deceptive subject headings, and includes an opt-out opportunity and other features that proponents argue will allow recipients to take control of their in-boxes. Proponents of the law argue that consumers will benefit because they should see a reduction in fraudulent e-mails. Opponents of the law counter that it legitimizes sending commercial e-mail, and to the extent that consumers do not want to receive such e-mails, the amount of unwanted e-mail actually may increase. If the legislation reduces the amount of fraudulent e-mail, but not the amount of unwanted e-mail, the extent to which it reduces "spam" would depend on what definition of that word is used.

In its June 2004 report to Congress on a National Do Not Email Registry (discussed below), the FTC referred to spam as unsolicited commercial e-mail.

AVOIDING AND REPORTING SPAM

Tips on avoiding spam are available on the FTC website [http://www.ftc.gov/ bcp/menu-internet.htm] and from Consumers Union [http://www.consumersunion.org/pub/core_product_safety/000210.html#mo re]. The September 2004 issue of *Consumer Reports* has a cover story about spam, including ratings of commercially available spam filters consumers can load onto their computers. Consumers may file a complaint about spam with the FTC by visiting the FTC website [http://www.ftc.gov] and choosing "File a Complaint" at the bottom of the page. The offending spam also may be forwarded to the FTC, at spam@uce.gov, to assist the FTC in monitoring spam trends and developments. Many ISPs use spam filters (though the filters may not catch all spam) and mechanisms for subscribers to report spam.

RESTRAINING SPAM: FEDERAL LAW — THE CAN-SPAM ACT

The 108th Congress passed the CAN-SPAM Act, S. 877, which merged provisions from several House and Senate bills.[10] Signed into law by President Bush on December 16, 2003 (P.L. 108-187), it went into effect on January 1, 2004.

The Senate originally passed S. 877 on October 22, 2003, by a vote of 97-0. As passed at that time, the bill[11] combined elements from several of the Senate bills. The House passed (392-5) an amended version of S. 877 on November 21, 2003, melding provisions from the Senate-passed bill and several House bills. The Senate concurred in the House amendment, with an amendment, on November 25, through unanimous consent. The Senate amendment included several revisions, requiring the House to vote again on the bill. The House agreed with the Senate amendment by unanimous consent on December 8, 2003.

Summary of the Major Provisions of the CAN-SPAM Act

The major provisions of P.L. 108-187 include the following.

- Commercial e-mail may be sent to recipients as long as the message conforms with the following requirements: — transmission information in the header is not false or misleading; — subject headings are not deceptive; — a functioning return e-mail address or comparable mechanism is included to enable recipients to indicate they do not wish to receive future commercial e-mail messages from that sender at the e-mail address where the message was received (**the "opt-out" requirement**); — the e-mail is not sent to a recipient by the sender, or anyone acting on behalf of the sender, more than 10 days after the recipient has opted-out, unless the recipient later gives affirmative consent to receive the e-mail (i.e., opts back in); and — the e-mail must be clearly and conspicuously identified as an advertisement or solicitation (although the legislation does not state how or where that identification must be made).

- Commercial e-mail is defined as e-mail, the primary purpose of which is the commercial advertisement or promotion of a commercial product or service (including content on an Internet website operated for a commercial purpose). It does not include transactional or relationship messages (see next bullet). The act directs the FTC to issue regulations within 12 months of enactment to define the criteria to facilitate determination of an e-mail's primary purpose. (See **Other FTC Implementation Actions** below for the status of that rulemaking activity.)

- Some requirements (including the prohibition on deceptive subject headings, and the opt-out requirement) do not apply if the message is a "transactional or relationship message," which include various types of notifications, such as periodic notifications of account balance or other information regarding a subscription, membership, account, loan or comparable ongoing commercial relationship involving the ongoing purchase or use by the recipient of products or services offered by the sender; providing information directly related to an employment relationship or related benefit plan in which the recipient is currently involved, participating, or enrolled; or delivering goods or services, including product updates or upgrades, that the recipient is entitled to receive under the terms of a transaction that the recipient has previously agreed to enter into with the sender. The act allows the FTC to modify that definition. (See **Other FTC Implementation Actions** for information on the status of that rulemaking activity.)

- Sexually oriented commercial e-mail must include, in the subject heading, a "warning label" to be prescribed by the FTC (in consultation with the Attorney General), indicating its nature. The warning label does not have to be in the subject line, however, if the message that is initially viewable by the recipient does not contain the sexually oriented material, but only a link to it. In that case, the warning label, and the identifier, opt-out, and physical address required under section 5 (a)(5) of the act; must be contained in the initially viewable e-mail message as well. Sexually oriented material is defined as any material that depicts sexually explicit conduct, unless the depiction constitutes a small and insignificant part of the whole, the remainder of which is not primarily devoted to sexual matters. These provisions do not apply, however, if the recipient has given prior affirmative consent to receiving such e-mails.

- Businesses may not knowingly promote themselves with e-mail that has false or misleading transmission information.
- State laws specifically related to spam are preempted, but not other state laws that are not specific to electronic mail, such as trespass, contract, or tort law, or other state laws to the extent they relate to fraud or computer crime.
- Violators may be sued by FTC, state attorneys general, and ISPs (but not by individuals).
- Violators of many of the provisions of the act are subject to statutory damages of up to $250 per e-mail, to a maximum of up to $2 million, which may be tripled by the court (to $6 million) for "aggravated violations."
- Violators may be fined, or sentenced to up to 3 or five years in prison (depending on the offense), or both, for accessing someone else's computer without authorization and using it to send multiple commercial e-mail messages; sending multiple commercial e-mail messages with the intent to deceive or mislead recipients or ISPs as to the origin of such messages; materially falsifying header information in multiple commercial e-mail messages; registering for 5 or more e-mail accounts or online user accounts, or 2 or more domain names, using information that materially falsifies the identity of the actual registrant, and sending multiple commercial e-mail messages from any combination of such accounts or domain names; or falsely representing oneself to be the registrant or legitimate successor in interest to the registrant of 5 of more Internet Protocol addresses, and sending multiple commercial e-mail messages from such addresses. "Multiple" means more than 100 e-mail messages during a 24-hour period, more than 1,000 during a 30-day period, or more than 10,000 during a one-year period. Sentencing enhancements are provided for certain acts.
- The Federal Communications Commission, in consultation with the FTC, must prescribe rules to protect users of wireless devices from unwanted commercial messages. (The rules were issued in August 2004. See CRS Report RL31636 for more on this topic.)

Conversely, the act does not —

- Create a "Do Not Email registry" where consumers can place their e-mail addresses in a centralized database to indicate they do not want commercial e-mail. The law requires only that the FTC develop a plan and timetable for establishing such a registry and to inform Congress of any concerns it has with regard to establishing it. (The FTC released that report in June 2004; see next section).
- Require that consumers "opt-in" before receiving commercial e-mail.
- Require commercial e-mail to include an identifier such as "ADV" in the subject line to indicate it is an advertisement. The law does require the FTC to report to Congress within 18 months of enactment on a plan for requiring commercial e-mail to be identifiable from its subject line through use of "ADV" or a comparable identifier, or compliance with Internet Engineering Task Force standards, or an explanation of any concerns FTC has about such a plan.
- Include a "bounty hunter" provision to financially reward persons who identify a violator and supply information leading to the collection of a civil penalty, although the FTC must submit a report to Congress within nine months of enactment setting forth a system for doing so. (The study was released in September 2004; see **Other FTC Implementation Actions** below).

Opt-In, Opt-Out, and a "Do Not Email" Registry

Discussion. Much of the debate on how to stop spam focuses on whether consumers should be given the opportunity to "opt-in" (where prior consent is required) or "opt-out" (where consent is assumed unless the consumer notifies the sender that such e-mails are not desired) of receiving UCE or all commercial e-mail. The CAN-SPAM Act is an "opt out" law, requiring senders of all commercial e-mail to provide a legitimate[12] opt-out opportunity to recipients.

During debate on the CAN-SPAM Act, several anti-spam groups argued that the legislation should go further, and prohibit commercial e-mail from being sent to recipients unless they opt-in, similar to a policy adopted by the European Union (see below). Eight U.S. groups, including Junkbusters, the Coalition Against Unsolicited Commercial Email (CAUCE), and the

Consumer Federation of America, wrote a letter to several Members of Congress expressing their view that the opt-out approach (as in P.L. 108-187) would "undercut those businesses who respect consumer preferences and give legal protection to those who do not."[13] Some of the state laws (see below) adopted the opt-in approach, including California's anti-spam law.

The European Union adopted an opt-in requirement for e-mail, which became effective October 31, 2003.[14] Under the EU policy, prior affirmative consent of the recipient must be obtained before sending commercial e-mail unless there is an existing customer relationship. In that case, the sender must provide an opt-out opportunity. The EU directive sets the broad policy, but each member nation must pass its own law as to how to implement it.[15]

As noted, Congress chose opt-out instead of opt-in, however. One method of implementing opt-out is to create a "Do Not Email" registry where consumers could place their names on a centralized list to opt-out of all commercial e-mail instead of being required to respond to individual e-mails. The concept is similar to the National Do Not Call registry where consumers can indicate they do not want to receive telemarketing calls. During consideration of the CAN-SPAM Act, then-FTC Chairman Timothy Muris and other FTC officials repeatedly expressed skepticism about the advisability of a Do Not Email registry despite widespread public support for it.[16] One worry is that the database containing the e-mail addresses of all those who do not want spam would be vulnerable to hacking, or spammers otherwise might be able to use it to obtain the e-mail addresses of individuals who explicitly do not want to receive spam. In an August 19, 2003, speech to the Aspen Institute, Mr. Muris commented that the concept of a Do Not Email registry was interesting, "but it is unclear how we can make it work" because it would not be enforceable.[17] "If it were established, my advice to consumers would be: Don't waste the time and effort to sign up."

Following initial Senate passage of S. 877, an unnamed FTC official was quoted by the *Washington Post* as saying that the FTC's position on the registry is unchanged, and "Congress would have to change the law" to require the FTC to create it.[18] After the House passed S. 877, Mr. Muris released a statement complimenting Congress on taking a positive step in the fight against spam, but cautioned again that legislation alone will not solve the problem.[19]

CAN-SPAM Act Provision. The CAN-SPAM Act did not require the FTC to create a Do Not Email registry.[20] Instead, it required the FTC to submit a plan and timetable for establishing a registry, authorized the FTC to create it, and instructed the FTC to explain to Congress any concerns about establishing it.

FTC Implementation. The FTC issued its report to Congress on June 15, 2004.[21] The report concluded that without a technical system to authenticate the origin of e-mail messages, a Do Not Email registry would not reduce the amount of spam, and, in fact, might increase it. (See below, **Restraining Spam — Non-Legislative Approaches**, for more on authentication.)

The FTC report stated that "spammers would most likely use a Registry as a mechanism for verifying the validity of e-mail addresses and, without authentication, the Commission would be largely powerless to identify those responsible for misusing the Registry. Moreover, a Registry-type solution to spam would raise serious security, privacy, and enforcement difficulties." (p. i) The report added that protecting children from "the Internet's most dangerous users, including pedophiles," would be difficult if the Registry identified accounts used by children in order to assist legitimate marketers from sending inappropriate messages to them. (p. i) The FTC described several registry models that had been suggested, and computer security techniques that some claimed would eliminate or alleviate security and privacy risks. The FTC stated that it carefully examined those techniques — a centralized scrubbing of marketers' distribution lists, converting addresses to one-way hashes (a cryptographic approach), and seeding the Registry with "canary" e-mail addresses — to determine if they could effectively control the risks "and has concluded that none of them would be effective." (p. 16)

The FTC concluded that a necessary prerequisite for a Do Not Email registry is an authentication system that prevents the origin of e-mail messages from being falsified, and proposed a program to encourage the adoption by industry of an authentication standard. If a single standard does not emerge from the private sector after a sufficient period of time, the FTC report said the Commission would initiate a process to determine if a federally mandated standard is required. If the government mandates a standard, the FTC would then consider studying whether an authentication system, coupled with enforcement or other mechanisms, had substantially reduced the amount of spam. If not, the Commission would then reconsider whether or not a Do Not Email registry is needed.

Labels

Discussion. Another approach to restraining spam is requiring that senders of commercial e-mail use a label, such as "ADV," in the subject line of the message, so the recipient will know before opening an e-mail message that it is an advertisement. That would also make it easier for spam filtering software to identify commercial e-mail and eliminate it. Some propose that adult-oriented spam have a special label, such as ADV-ADLT, to highlight that the e-mail may contain material or links that are inappropriate for children, such as pornography.

CAN-SPAM Act Provision. The CAN-SPAM Act: (1) requires clear and conspicuous identification that a commercial e-mail is an advertisement, but is not specific about how or where that identification must be made; (2) requires the FTC to prescribe warning labels for sexually-oriented e-mails within 120 days of enactment; and (3) requires the FTC to submit a report within 18 months of enactment setting forth a plan for requiring commercial e-mail to be identifiable from its subject line using ADV or a comparable identifier, or by means of compliance with Internet Engineering Task Force standards. However, the clear and conspicuous identification that a commercial e-mail is an advertisement, and the warning label for sexually-oriented material, are not required if the recipient has given prior affirmative consent to receipt of such messages.

FTC Implementation. On May 19, 2004, an FTC rule regarding labeling of sexually oriented commercial e-mail went into effect. The rule was adopted by the FTC (5-0) on April 13, 2004. A press release and the text of the ruling are available on the FTC's website at [http://www.ftc.gov/opa/2004/04/adultlabel.htm]. The rule requires that the mark "SEXUALLY-EXPLICIT" be included both in the subject line of any commercial e-mail containing sexually oriented material, and in the body of the message in what the FTC called the "electronic equivalent of a 'brown paper wrapper.'" The FTC explained that the "brown paper wrapper" is what a recipient initially sees when opening the e-mail, and it may not contain any other information or images except what the FTC prescribes. The rule also clarifies that the FTC interprets the CAN-SPAM Act provisions to include both visual images and written descriptions of sexually explicit conduct.

Other FTC Implementation Actions

The FTC is working on other issues identified in the act. In March 2004, the FCC requested comments through an Advance Notice of Proposed Rulemaking [http://www.ftc.gov/opa/2004/03/canspam.htm] on these topics:

- how to define the relevant criteria to facilitate determination of an e-mail's "primary purpose";
- whether to modify the definition of "transactional or relationship messages";
- whether to modify the 10-day time period specified in the act within which an opt-out request must be honored; and
- what activities and practices, if any, should be added to the list of aggravated violations specified in the act; any additional regulations that might be needed to help implement the act.

A Notice of Proposed Rulemaking on the first question — defining the primary purpose of a commercial e-mail — was announced on August 11, 2004; comments were due by September 13, 2004.

The act also required the FTC to conduct a study on whether rewarding persons who identify a spammer and supply information leading to the collection of a civil penalty could be an effective technique for controlling spam (the "bounty hunter" provision). The study was released on September 15, 2004.[22] The FTC concluded that the benefits of such a system are unclear because, for example, without large rewards (in the $100,000 to $250,000 range) and a certain level of assurance that they would receive the reward, whistleblowers might not be willing to assume the risks of providing such information. The FTC offered five recommendations if Congress wants to pursue such an approach:

- tie eligibility for a reward to imposition of a final court order, instead of to collecting a civil penalty;
- fund the rewards through congressional appropriations, instead of through collected civil penalties;
- restrict reward eligibility to insiders with high-value information;
- exempt FTC decisions on eligibility for rewards from judicial or administrative review; and
- establish reward amounts high enough to attract insiders with high-value information.

The CAN-SPAM Act also required the Federal Communications Commission (FCC) to issue regulations concerning spam on wireless devices such as cell phones. The FCC issued those regulations in August 2004. See CRS Report RL31636 for more information.

Legal Actions Based on the CAN-SPAM Act

On April 29, 2004, the FTC announced that it had filed a civil lawsuit against a Detroit-based spam operation, Phoenix Avatar, and the Department of Justice (DOJ) announced that it had arrested two (and were seeking two more) Detroit-area men associated with the company who are charged with sending hundreds of thousands of spam messages using false and fraudulent headers.[23] The FTC charged Phoenix Avatar with making deceptive claims about a diet patch sold via the spam in violation of the FTC Act, and with violations of the CAN-SPAM Act because the spam did not contain a valid opt-out opportunity and the "reply to" and "from" addresses were fraudulent. The DOJ filed criminal charges against the men under the CAN-SPAM Act for sending multiple commercial e-mails with materially false or fraudulent return addresses. According to the FTC, since January 1, 2004, among the spam forwarded by consumers to the FTC, about 490,000 were linked to Avatar Phoenix.

The FTC simultaneously announced that it had filed a legal action against an Australian spam enterprise operating out of Australia and New Zealand called Global Web Promotions. The FTC stated that it was assisted by the Australian Competition and Consumer Commission and the New Zealand Commerce Committee in bringing the case. According to the FTC, since January 1, 2004, among the spam forwarded by consumers to the FTC, about 399,000 are linked to Global Web Promotions. The FTC charges that a diet patch, and human growth hormone products, sold by Global Web Promotions are deceptive and in violation of the FTC Act. The products are shipped from within the United States. The FTC further charges that the spam violates the CAN-SPAM Act because of fraudulent headers.

Separately, four of the largest ISPs — AOL, Earthlink, Microsoft, and Yahoo! — filed civil suits under the CAN-SPAM Act against hundreds of alleged spammers in March 2004.[24] The suits were filed in federal courts in California, Georgia, Virginia and Washington. Additional CAN-SPAM suits since have been filed, including one by the Massachusetts Attorney General against a Florida business called DC Enterprises, and its proprietor William T. Carson.[25]

Reaction to and Effectiveness of the CAN-SPAM Act

Both praise and criticism greeted enactment of the CAN-SPAM Act. Among those praising the law are marketing groups such as the DMA,[26] ISPs such as America Online,[27] and Microsoft chairman Bill Gates.[28] Generally, they support a single federal law, instead of a "patchwork quilt" of state laws, and legislation that permits "legitimate" commercial e-mail while taking measures against fraudulent e-mail. The DMA did express reservations, however, about the provision authorizing the FTC to create a "Do Not Email" registry, even though the law does not, in fact, require the FTC to do so.

Some commercial e-mailers also appeared pleased. For example, Scott Richter, the president of an e-mail marketing firm in Colorado, expressed relief that the federal law preempted a stricter California law that was slated to become effective January 1, 2004 (discussed below).[29]

Critics include those who wanted opt-in legislation, including advocates of California's opt-in law. California State Senator Debra Bowen was quoted as saying that the CAN-SPAM Act, "... doesn't can spam. It legalizes it.... It's full of loopholes. It's difficult to enforce. It's weaker than many state laws."[30] The Coalition Against Unsolicited Commercial E-Mail (CAUCE) expressed disappointment with the final version of the law, saying that it "fails the most fundamental test of any anti-spam law, in that it neglects to actually tell any marketers not to spam."[31] Another criticism is that the law does not allow individuals to sue spammers, only the FTC, ISPs, and state attorneys general can sue.

The law's effectiveness in reducing spam is likely to be the subject of debate, particularly in the near term while lawsuits are pending. One of the bill's sponsors, Senator Conrad Burns, acknowledged that "I don't think you will see really a cutback in spam until someone is caught and prosecuted and they know for sure that we are serious about the enforcement of the law...."[32] Overall, the extent to which it reduces "spam" depends in part on how that word is defined. Some consider spam to be only fraudulent commercial e-mail, and anticipate that the civil and criminal penalties in the law may reduce the volume of that type of commercial e-mail. Others consider spam to be any unsolicited commercial e-mail, and since the law permits commercial e-mail to be sent as long as it complies with the law's requirements, they argue that consumers may see an increase, not a decrease, in commercial e-mail.

A survey of 2,000 e-mail users released by Consumers Union (CU) in August 2004 found that spam comprised more than half of the e-mail of 69%

of the respondents, and, three months after the law went into effect, 47% said
that they were receiving more spam, not less.[33] CU President Jim Guest
was quoted by the *Wall Street Journal* as saying that the law was inadequate,
and opt-in should have been required. He reportedly criticized attempts to
distinguish between fraudulent spam and unsolicited advertising from
legitimate marketers: "'Spam is spam and consumers don't want any of it,'
he said."[34]

Statistics from Brightmail also indicate that the percentage of spam in
Internet e-mail continues to grow.[35] However, an America Online (AOL)
official reported on March 19, 2004, that the company experienced a 27%
drop in spam since February 20, 2004.[36]

RESTRAINING SPAM: STATE LAWS

According to the SpamLaws website [http://www.spamlaws.com], 36
states passed laws regulating spam: Alaska, Arizona, Arkansas, California,
Colorado, Connecticut, Delaware, Idaho, Illinois, Indiana, Iowa, Kansas,
Louisiana, Maine, Maryland, Michigan, Minnesota, Missouri, Nevada, New
Mexico, North Carolina, North Dakota, Ohio, Oklahoma, Oregon,
Pennsylvania, Rhode Island, South Dakota, Tennessee, Texas, Utah,
Virginia, Washington, West Virginia, Wisconsin, and Wyoming. The
specifics of each law varies. Summaries of and links to each law are
provided on that website. CRS Report RL31488, *Regulation of Unsolicited
Commercial E-Mail*, provides a brief review of the state laws and challenges
to them.

The CAN-SPAM Act preempts state spam laws, but not other state laws
that are not specific to electronic mail, such as trespass, contract, or tort law,
or other state laws to the extent they relate to fraud or computer crime.
California passed an anti-spam law that would have become effective
January 1, 2004 and was considered relatively strict. It required opt-in for
UCE unless there was a prior business relationship, in which case, opt-out is
required. The anticipated implementation of that California law is often cited
as one of the factors that stimulated Congress to complete action on a less
restrictive, preemptive federal law before the end of 2003.[37]

RESTRAINING SPAM:
NON-LEGISLATIVE APPROACHES

As discussed above, the extent to which the law will restrain spam is not clear. Even before the law was passed, many cautioned that legislation alone is insufficient. Senator McCain, for example, was quoted as saying that he supported the passage of legislation, but is not optimistic about its effect: "I'll support it, report it, vote for it, take credit for it, but will it make much difference? I don't think so."[38]

During 2003, in congressional testimony and other speeches, then-FTC Chairman Muris repeatedly argued that a combination of legislation, technological advancements, and consumer education is needed. Calling spam "one of the most daunting consumer protection problems that the Commission has ever faced ," he noted that "Despite the concerted efforts of government regulators, Internet service providers, and other interested parties, the problem continues to worsen."[39] During congressional debate on the CAN-SPAM Act, the White House, and the Departments of Justice and Commerce also warned that federal legislation alone cannot solve the spam problem — that development and adoption of new technologies also is needed.[40,41]

Mr. Muris cited two significant differences between spam and other types of marketing. First, spammers can easily hide their identities and cross international borders. Second, sending additional spam "is essentially costless" to the spammer; the cost is borne by ISPs and recipients instead. This "cost shifting" means there is no incentive to the spammer to reduce the volume of messages being sent, and a bulk e-mailer testified at an FTC forum on spam that he could profit even if his response rate was less than 0.0001%.[42]

ISPs are motivated to reduce spam because they want to retain subscribers who might weary of spam and abandon e-mail entirely, reduce the need to upgrade server capacity to cope with the traffic, and avoid the costs associated with litigation. Though lawsuits may be costly, for the past several years, ISPs have, in fact, taken spammers to court using laws that existed prior to the CAN-SPAM Act. As noted above, America Online, Earthlink, Microsoft, and Yahoo! filed lawsuits under the provisions of the CAN-SPAM Act in March 2004. But the ISPs continue to look for new approaches to reducing spam. Those four ISPs are also working together through the Anti-Spam Technical Alliance to devise technological measures to address spam, as discussed below.

Spam filters are widely used today by ISPs, corporations, universities, and other organizations. Spammers are aware of that, however, and routinely find methods for defeating the filters by misspelling words, using symbols instead of letters, or "spoofing" the return address (spoofing is discussed below). Coupled with the fact that the filters may inadvertently block wanted e-mails, they are not considered an ideal solution. Some of the other non-legislative approaches to reducing spam are described below.

Securing Internet Connections

Spammers increasingly are taking advantage of "always on" Internet connections, such as cable modems or Digital Subscriber Lines (DSL), belonging to consumers who are unaware that spam is being routed through their computers. In a January 2004 consumer alert entitled "Who's Spamming Who? Could it Be You?," the FTC called on consumers to be vigilant about securing their computers by using firewalls and anti-virus software, being cautious in opening e-mail attachments from unknown senders, and taking other steps.[43] The FTC estimated that 30% of all spam is sent by compromised computers — called "zombies" — in home offices and living rooms. Comcast reportedly has begun blocking access to "port 25," through which home and small business customers can send e-mail directly to the Internet instead of through Comcast servers, because some of those accounts are being used for spam. It is not blocking all access to Port 25; only for those customers whose computers are sending suspicious amounts of e-mail. Some critics have called for Port 25 to be completely blocked by all ISPs. Richard Wong, of Openwave Systems and the Messaging Anti-Abuse Working Group, estimates that one-third of ISPs block port 25, and another third are considering it.[44] The Anti-Spam Technical Alliance, which includes Microsoft, AOL, Yahoo!, and Earthlink, called for ISPs and E-mail Service Providers (ESPs) to block or limit use of Port 25.[45]

In addition, the FTC and regulatory agencies in more than two dozen countries announced "Operation Secure Your Server" in January 2004,[46] an effort to close "open relays" or "open proxies" in businesses that similarly can be used by spammers to reroute their messages and thereby disguise their origin. The agencies sent letters to "tens of thousands" of owners or operators of servers that might be used in this manner urging them to take steps to protect their computers from misuse.

Authentication

Another alternative is to require senders to "authenticate" who they are so that recipients may determine whether or not it is spam. As the FTC report on the National Do Not Email Registry explained, when an e-mail message is transmitted from a sender's computer to a recipient's computer, the Simple Mail Transfer Protocol (SMTP) requires only that the receiving computer verify that a valid transmission is being received, not whether the "servername" is the actual name of the sending computer. That is, the receiving computer does not require authentication of the sending computer. The only piece of information which must be accurate is the recipient's address. Others steps in the e-mail process similarly do not require authentication.[47]

There are a variety of approaches to authentication.

Challenge-Response. "Challenge-response" software is one method of authentication. It requires the sender to respond to an action requested in an automatically generated return e-mail before the original e-mail reaches the intended recipient. Challenge-response is based on the concept that spammers are sending e-mail with automated systems that cannot read a return e-mail and respond to a question (such as "how many kittens are in this picture"), but a person can, so if the e-mail was sent by an individual rather than a bulk e-mail system, the person will answer the question or perform a requested action and the e-mail will be delivered. Earthlink offers this option to its subscribers. It is not clear to what extent such software may become popular, however. *Business Week* outlined some of the potential unintended consequences, including recipients not receiving confirmation of orders placed over the Internet (which often are generated by automated systems), and difficulty if the sender is using an Internet-access device that does not display graphics (e.g., a Blackberry) or is visually impaired.[48]

Microsoft's Three-Part Strategy: "Caller ID," Certificates, and "Postage". In a February 24, 2004 speech,[49] Microsoft Corp. Chairman Bill Gates detailed three initiatives for dealing with the spam problem.

One of the initiatives deals with "spoofing," where spammers use false addresses — often legitimate e-mail addresses that the spammer obtained through legitimate or illegitimate means — in the "from" line to avoid spam filters and deceive recipients into opening the message. Mr. Gates announced that his company would pilot test a **"Caller ID for E-Mail"** system to enable ISPs to determine if a "from" line is spoofed. He said that Microsoft would make available a list of all the numeric Internet addresses assigned to Microsoft computers that send out mail. Other ISPs would then be able to check an incoming message purporting to be from a Microsoft computer to determine if that actually was its origin. If not, then the message would be blocked. Mr. Gates envisioned other e-mail senders similarly making their numeric addresses known in order to implement the system broadly. He noted that Brightmail, Amazon.com, and Sendmail Inc. were working with Microsoft on this initiative. Microsoft subsequently reached agreement to merge its Caller ID with another authentication method, Sender Policy Framework (SPF), yielding "Sender ID," which is discussed below.

For "legitimate" high-volume e-mail senders, Microsoft proposed an approach similar to what was implemented in the Internet privacy arena, where certain organizations offer "seals of approval" to websites that abide by certain privacy principles. These "seals" are offered by organizations such as the Better Business Bureau Online (BBB Online), WebTrust, or TRUSTe.[50] Microsoft proposed a similar regime where trusted entities would establish "reasonable behavior" practices, and issue a **certificate** that would indicate to a recipient or a spam filter that the sender is not a spammer. The marketers reportedly would fund the certificate system and pay for the certificates.[51]

The concept of requiring e-mail senders to pay **postage** for their messages, analogous to traditional mail service, has been broached for several years on the premise that it would increase the costs to spammers of sending out their messages, making spamming less economical. Since the postage would probably apply to all e-mail senders, however, there are concerns that it would restrain the use of e-mail, and the concept has not been widely embraced. However, Microsoft proposed a variation wherein rather than paying money, the sender would be required to devote a certain amount of computer processing time to each message as a demonstration that it is not spam. Mr. Gates views this approach as beneficial to legitimate small volume e-mail senders. The concept is based on the assumption that spammers send millions of messages a day, spending only a fraction of a second on each message, but that legitimate small-volume e-mail senders would have "an abundance of computer processing power available. Although they can't afford to spend cash for a certificate, they can afford to spend a few seconds on each message."[52] Microsoft did not rule out the possibility of requiring a financial payment, however, which it called a "micropayment."[53] Details were not provided.

FTC's Four Step Plan for Creating an Authentication Standard. The FTC report on a National Do Not Email Registry (cited earlier) discussed ongoing industry efforts at developing authentication standards. In addition to Microsoft's Caller ID for Email initiative, the Commission reported on a standard developed by Meng Weng Wong called Sender Policy Framework (SPF),[54] Yahoo!'s proposal for "domain keys," and efforts by an Internet Engineering Task Force (IETF) working group. The FTC noted that estimates vary widely as to when e-mail authentication will be reality: "Some believe that all e-mail will be authenticated within a year. Others are less sanguine."[55]

The Commission expressed its view that the marketplace should be given an opportunity to test and phase-in an authentication standard, but added that the pace might be accelerated by Commission support. The report identified several areas where its support might be beneficial, such as focusing efforts so that smaller ISPs and businesses, and individuals with their own domains, can ultimately use the standard, and in evaluating the international implications of the standard. It proposed a four-step plan: conducting a two-day "Authentication Summit"in the fall of 2004; convening a Federal Advisory Committee to help the FTC develop an authentication system if industry fails to produce a standard after a "sufficient" time; mandating the use of an authentication standard if industry does not adopt one itself; and subsequently evaluating whether the mandatory standard, combined with enforcement actions, is effective in reducing spam. If the answer to the last question is no, the Commission would reconsider the need to create a Do Not Email registry.

"Sender ID": A Merger of SPF and Caller ID. On June 22, 2004, Microsoft announced that it had reached agreement with Meng Weng Wong to merge his SPF standard with Microsoft's Caller ID proposal into a standard called "Sender ID." According to the Microsoft press release, in Sender ID, organizations would publish information about their outgoing e-mail servers (such as IP addresses) in the Domain Name System using XML format. Backward compatibility for the 20,000 domains that already have published information in SPF's TXT format would be provided. Microsoft's announcement stated that the converged standard would enable receiving systems to test for spoofing at both the message transport (SMTP) level used by SPF, and in message body headers, as proposed in Caller ID.

The Sender ID proposal was submitted to the IETF for consideration as an industry-wide standard.[56] The IETF working group reportedly rejected it, however, because of patent and licensing issues.[57] AOL subsequently announced that it was withdrawing its support for Sender ID and would rely instead on SPF.[58]

Table 1. Major Provisions of the CAN-SPAM Act

Provision	P.L. 108-187 (S. 877)
Title	Controlling the Assault of Non-Solicited Pornography and Marketing (CAN-SPAM) Act
Definition of Commercial E-Mail	E-mail whose primary purpose is commercial advertisement or promotion of commercial product or service, with exceptions.
	Transactional or relationship message (as defined in the act) is not commercial e-mail.
	FTC shall issue regulations within 12 months after enactment further defining the relevant criteria to facilitate the determination of the "primary purpose" of a commercial e-mail message.
Definition of Unsolicited Commercial E-mail	Not defined.
Creates "Do Not Email" registry at FTC	No, but requires FTC to submit to Congress, within six months of enactment, plan and timetable for creating such a registry; to explain any concerns it has about creating it; and to explain how it would be applied with respect to children. Authorizes (but does not require) FTC to establish and implement the plan.
Prohibits deceptive subject headings	Yes, in all commercial e-mail.
Prohibits false, misleading, or deceptive information in body of message	No, but does not affect FTC's authority to bring enforcement actions for materially false or deceptive representations in commercial e-mail.
Prohibits transmission of e-mail from improperly or illegally harvested e-mail addresses	Yes, in commercial e-mail prohibited under other sections of the act.
	Also prohibits dictionary attacks, and using automated means to register for multiple e-mail or on-line user accounts from which to transmit, or enable someone else to transmit unlawful commercial e-mail as defined by the act.
Prohibits sending e-mails through computers accessed without authorization	Prohibits accessing a computer without authorization and transmitting multiple commercial e-mail messages from or through it.
Prohibits businesses from knowingly promoting themselves with e-mail that has false or misleading transmission information	Yes

Table 1. continued

Provision	P.L. 108-187 (S. 877)
Penalties for falsifying sender's identity	Yes
Requires FTC-prescribed "warning labels" on sexually oriented material	Yes, unless recipient has given prior affirmative consent to receipt of the message.
Requires specific characters in subject line to indicate the message is an advertisement	No, but commercial e-mail must provide clear and conspicuous identification that it is an advertisement, but not if the recipient has given prior affirmative consent to receive the message. Also, FTC must report to Congress within 18 months of enactment on plan for requiring commercial e-mail to be identifiable from its subject line through use of "ADV" or comparable identifier, or compliance with Internet Engineering Task Force standards, or an explanation of any concerns FTC has about such a plan.
Requires opt-out mechanism	Commercial e-mail must provide clear and conspicuous notice of opportunity to opt-out, and functioning e-mail return address or other Internet-based mechanism to which the recipient may opt-out. Sender cannot send commercial e-mail to recipient more than 10 days after recipient has opted out. Sender, or anyone acting on sender's behalf, cannot sell, lease, exchange, or otherwise transfer recipient's e-mail address for any purpose other than compliance with this act or if the recipient has given express consent. Opt out does not apply if recipient later opts back in by affirmative consent.
Damages or Penalties	Civil and criminal penalties; vary per violation.
Reward for first person identifying a violator and supplying information leading to the collection of a civil penalty	No, but requires FTC to transmit a report to Congress within nine months of enactment that sets forth a system for rewarding those who supply information about violations, including granting a reward of not less than 20% of civil penalty collected.
Private Right of Action	For ISPs only.

Table 1. continued

Provision	P.L. 108-187 (S. 877)
Affirmative Defense/Safe Harbor	No, but in assessing damages, courts may consider whether defendant established and implemented, with due care, reasonable practices and procedures to effectively prevent violations, or the violation occurred despite commercially reasonable efforts to maintain compliance with such practices and procedures.
Enforcement	By FTC, except for certain entities that are regulated by other agencies.
State action allowed	Yes, but must notify FTC or other appropriate regulator, which may intervene.
Effect on ISPs	ISPs may bring civil action in U.S. district court. Does not affect the lawfulness or unlawfulness under other laws of ISP policies declining to transmit, route, relay, handle, or store certain types of e-mail.
Supersedes state and local laws and regulations	Yes, but does not preempt other state laws that are not specific to electronic mail, such as trespass, contract, or tort law, or other state laws to the extent that they relate to fraud or computer crime.
Provisions regarding spam on wireless devices	Requires Federal Communications Commission, in consultation with FTC, to promulgate rules within 270 days of enactment to protect consumers from unwanted mobile service commercial messages.

Aspen Summit, Aspen, CP, August 19, 2003. [http://www.ftc.gov/speeches/muris/030819aspen.htm].

[18] Krim, Jonathan. Senate Votes 97-0 to Restrict E-Mail Ads; Bill Could Lead to No-Spam Registry. Washington Post, October 23, 2003, p. A1 (via Factiva).

[19] U.S. Federal Trade Commission. Statement of Timothy J. Muris Regarding Passage of the Can-Spam Act of 2003. November 21, 2003. [http://www.ftc.gov/opa/2003/11/spamstmt.htm]

[20] The FTC issued a warning to consumers in February 2004 that a website (unsub.us) promoting a National Do Not Email Registry is a sham and might be collecting e-mail addresses to sell to spammers. See [http://www.ftc.gov/opa/2004/02/spamcam.htm].

[21] U.S. Federal Trade Commission. National Do Not Email Registry: A Report to Congress. Washington, FTC, June 2004. A press release, and a link to the report, is available at [http://www.ftc.gov/opa/2004/06/canspam2.htm].

[22] A press release is available at [http://www.ftc.gov/opa/2004/09/bounty.htm], and the report, A CAN-Spam Informant Reward System, is available at [http://www.ftc.gov/reports/rewardsys/040916reward sysrpt.pdf].

[23] FTC Announces First Can-Spam Act Cases. [http://www.ftc.gov/opa/2004/04/040429canspam.htm]; (2) Department of Justice Announces Arrests of Detroit-Area Men on Violations of the 'Can-Spam' Act. [http://www.usdoj.gov/opa/pr/2004/April/04_crm_281.htm].

[24] Mangalindan, Mylene. Web Firms File Spam Suit Under New Law. Wall Street Journal, March 11, 2004, p. B4, via Factiva.

[25] Hines, Matt. Massachusetts Files Suit Under Can-Spam. C|NET News.com, July 2, 2004, 11:54 am PDT.

[26] Direct Marketing Association. Senate Updates Spam Bill; Must Return to House for Final Action. News Release, November 25, 2003 [http://www.the-dma.org/cgi/dispnewsstand?article=1662+++++]

[27] America Online, an Industry Leader in the Fight for Tougher Anti-Spam Laws, Applauds Bipartisan Congressional Agreement and Action on Tough New Spam Laws, America Online, Press Release November 21, 2003 [http://media.aoltimewarner.com/media/new media/ cb_press_view.cfm?release_num=552 53625]

[28] Gates, Bill. A Spam-Free Future. Washington Post, November 24, 2003, p. A 21 (via Factiva).

[29] Quoted in: Andrews, Edmund L. and Saul Hansell. Congress Set to Pass Bill That Restrains Unsolicited E-Mail. New York Times, November 22, 2003, p. 1 (via Factiva).

[30] Quoted in: Lee, Jennifer B. Antispam Bill Passes Senate by Voice Vote. New York Times, November 26, 2003, p. 3 (via Factiva).

[31] CAUCE Statement on House and Senate Spam Bill Vote. November 25, 2003. Available at [http://www.cauce.org/news/index.shtml].

[32] Quoted in: Lee, Jennifer B. Antispam Bill Passes Senate by Voice Vote. New York Times, November 26, 2003, p. 3 (via Factiva).

[33] Consumers Union. Consumer Reports Investigates How to Protect Against Spam, Spyware and Phishing. Press Release, August 9, 20004. [http://www.consumersunion.org/pub/core_product_safety/00 1305.html#more]

[34] Nasaw, Daniel. Federal Law Fails to Lessen Flow of Junk E-Mail. Wall Street Journal, August 10, 2004, p. D2 (via Factiva).

[35] Statistics available at [http://www.brightmail.com] show the amount of spam as a percentage of all Internet e-mail was 58% in December 2003, just prior to the law becoming effective, and 65% in July 2004.

[36] Sullivan, Andy. AOL Says It Sees Sharp Decline in 'Spam' E-Mail. Reuters, March 19, 2004, 13:18 (via Factiva).

[37] For example, see Glanz, William. House Oks Measure Aimed at Spammers; Senate Likely to Approve Changes. Washington Times, November 22, 2003, p. A1 (via Factiva).

[38] Taylor, Chris. Spam's Big Bang. Time, June 16, 2003, p. 52.

[39] Muris, Aspen Summit speech, op. cit.

[40] Statement of Administration Policy. S. 877. Available at [http://www.whitehouse.gov/omb/legislative/sap/index-date.html]. Scroll down to S. 877.

[41] U.S. Department of Justice. Joint Statement of the Departments of Justice and Commerce on E-Mail Spam Legislation. Press Release 03-643. November 21, 2003. Available at [http://www.usdoj.gov/opa/pr/2003/November/03_opa_643.htm]

[42] Muris, Aspen Summit speech, op. cit.

[43] See [http://www.ftc.gov/bcp/conline/pubs/alerts/whospamalrt.htm].

[44] Krim, Jonathan. Comcast Slows Flow of Spam; ISP Limits Access to Abused Gateway. Washington Post, June 12, 2004, p. D12 (via Factiva).

[45] Microsoft Corp. Anti-Spam Technical Alliance Publishes Industry Recommendations to Help Stop Spam. Press Release, J une 22, 2004.

[http://www.microsoft.com/presspass/press/2004/jun04/06-22ASTAPR.asp].

[46] See [http://www.ftc.gov/secureyourserver/]. The other countries participating in this effort are: Albania, Argentina, Australia, Brazil, Bulgaria, Canada, Chile, Colombia, Denmark, Ecuador, Finland, Hungary, Jamaica, Japan, Lithuania, Norway, Panama, Peru, Romania, Serbia, Singapore, South Korea, Switzerland, Taiwan, and the United Kingdom.

[47] FTC National Do Not Email Registry report, op. cit., pp. 4-8 describe how the e-mail system works.

[48] Wildstrom, Stephen H. A Spam-Fighter More Noxious Than Spam. *Business Week*, July 7, 2003, p. 21.

[49] Gates, Bill. Remarks to RSA Conference 2004. The speech itself is at [http://www.microsoft.com/billgates/speeches/2004/02-24rsa.asp]. A Microsoft Corp. press release summarizing it is available at [http://www.microsoft.com/presspass/press/2004/feb04/02-24RSAAntiSpamTechVision PR.asp].

[50] See CRS Report RL31408, Internet Privacy: Overview and Pending Legislation, for more on Internet privacy seals.

[51] Krim, Jonathan. Microsoft to Launch Plan to Control Spam. Washington Post, February 25, 2004, p. E1 (via Factiva).

[52] Microsoft Corp. February 24, 2004 press release, op. cit.

[53] Microsoft Corp. Q&A: Microsoft's Anti-Spam Technology Roadmap. Press release, February 24, 2004. Available at [http://www.microsoft.com/presspass/features/2004/Feb04/02-24CallerID.asp].

[54] For more on SPF, see [http://spf.pobox.com/].

[55] FTC National Do Not Email Registry report, op. cit., p. 13

[56] Microsoft Corp. Sender ID Specification Submitted for Standards Body Consideration. Press Release, June 22, 2002. [http://www.microsoft.com/presspass/press/2004/jun04/06-24SIDSpecIETFPR.asp].

[57] Stevenson, Reed. Microsoft Issues Patch—E-mail ID Plan Rejected. Reuters, September 14, 2004, 16:07 (via Factiva).

[58] Wagner, Jim. AOL Dumps Sender ID. Internetnews.com, September 15, 2004 [http://www.internetnews.com/xSP/article.php/3408601].

[59] Krim, Jonathan. AOL Blocks Spammers' Web Sites. Washington Post, March 20, 2004, p. A1 (via Factiva).

In: Spam and Internet Privacy
Editor: B.G. Kutais, pp. 31-37

Chapter 2

"JUNK E-MAIL": AN OVERVIEW OF ISSUES AND LEGISLATION CONCERNING UNSOLICITED COMMERCIAL ELECTRONIC MAIL ("SPAM")[*]

Marcia S. Smith

SUMMARY

Unsolicited commercial e-mail (UCE), also called "spam" or "junk e-mail," aggravates many computer users. Not only can it be a nuisance, but its cost may be passed on to consumers through higher charges from Internet service providers who must upgrade their systems to handle the traffic. Proponents of UCE insist it is a legitimate marketing technique and protected by the First Amendment. Legislation to place limits on UCE was considered by the last three Congresses (105th-107th), but no federal law was enacted (27 states have anti-spam laws, however). Two bills have been introduced in the 108th Congress: S. 563 (Dayton) and S. 877 (Burns). This report will be updated.

---

[*] Excerpted from CRS Report RS20037, Updated April 15, 2003

OVERVIEW

One aspect of increased use of the Internet for electronic mail (e-mail) has been the advent of unsolicited advertising, also called "unsolicited commercial e-mail (UCE)," "unsolicited bulk e-mail," "junk e-mail, "or "spam."[1] Issues involved in the debate are reviewed in *Report to the Federal Trade Commission of the Ad-Hoc Working Group on Unsolicited Commercial Email* [http://www.cdt.org/spam].

Consumers may file a complaint about spam with the Federal Trade Commission (FTC) by visiting the FTC Web site [http://www.ftc.gov] and scrolling down to "complaint form" at the bottom of the page. The offending spam also may be forwarded to the FTC (UCE@ftc.gov) to assist the FTC in monitoring UCE trends and developments. Three consumer publications are available on the FTC Web site [http://www.ftc.gov/opa/ 1999/9911/spam.htm]. Separately, CNET.com, a non-government site, has tips for consumers on how to protect themselves from spam at [http://home.cnet.com/internet/0-3793-8-5181225-1.html].

In 1991, Congress passed the Telephone Consumer Protection Act (P.L. 102-243) that prohibits, *inter alia*, unsolicited advertising via facsimile machines, or "junk fax" (see CRS Report RL30763, *Telemarketing: Dealing with Unwanted Telephone Calls*). Many think there should be an analogous law for computers, or some method for letting a consumer know before opening an e-mail message whether or not it is UCE and how to direct the sender to cease transmission of such messages. According to Brightmail, a company that sells anti-spam software, about 40% of all e-mail traffic is spam (*Washington Post*, March 13, 2003, p. 1.)

Opponents of junk e-mail argue that not only is it annoying and an invasion of privacy,[2] but that its cost is borne by consumers, not marketers. Consumers reportedly are charged higher fees by Internet service providers that must invest resources to upgrade equipment to manage the high volume of e-mail, deal with customer complaints, and mount legal challenges to junk e-mailers. Consumers also may incur costs for the time spent reading and/or deleting such e-mail. Some want to prevent bulk e-mailers from sending messages to anyone with whom they do not have an established business relationship, treating junk e-mail the same way as junk fax. The Coalition Against Unsolicited Commercial Email (CAUCE) [http://www.cauce.org] is one group opposing spam. Its founder, Ray Everett-Church, was cited in the January 31, 2001 edition of *Newsday* as saying that some Internet Service Providers (ISPs) estimate that spam costs consumers about $2-3 per month. The European Commission estimates that Internet subscribers globally pay

10 billion Euros a year in connection costs to download spam [http://europa.eu.int/comm/internal_market/en/dataprot/studies/spam.htm]. Proponents of UCE argue that it is a valid method of advertising. The Direct Marketing Association (DMA), for example, argued for several years that instead of banning UCE, individuals should be given the opportunity to "opt-out" by notifying the sender that they want to be removed from the mailing list. Hoping to demonstrate that self regulation could work, in January 2000, the DMA launched the E-mail Preference Service where consumers who wish to opt-out can register themselves at a DMA Web site [http://www.e-mps.org]. DMA members sending UCE must check their lists of recipients and delete those who have opted out. Critics argue that most spam does not come from DMA members, so the plan is insufficient. On October 20, 2002, the DMA agreed it was insufficient, announcing that it would pursue legislation to battle the rising volume of spam. A DMA official said spam must be curbed "to preserve the promise of e-mail as the next great marketing channel" [http://www.the-dma.org/cgi/disppressrelease?article=354].

To date, the issue of restraining junk e-mail has been fought primarily over the Internet or in the courts. Some Internet service providers (ISPs) will return junk e-mail toits origin, and groups opposed to junk e-mail will send blasts of e-mail to a mass e-mail company, disrupting the company's computer systems. Filtering software also is available to screen out e-mail based on keywords or return addresses. Knowing this, mass e-mailers may avoid certain keywords or continually change addresses to foil the software, however. In the courts, ISPs with unhappy customers and businesses that believe their reputations have been tarnished by misrepresentations in junk e-mail have brought suit against mass e-mailers.

Some UCE either contains indecent material or links to Web sites where indecent material is available. Thus, controls over junk e-mail have also arisen in the context of protecting children from unsuitable material. Other spam involves fraud. On February 12, 2002, the FTC announced that seven defendants caught in an FTC sting involving illegal chain letters had agreed to settle charges, and that it was mailing warning letters to more than 2,000 individuals still involved in the chain letter scheme (the FTC press release is available at [http://www.ftc.gov/opa/2002/02/eileenspam1.htm].

State Action

Although the U.S. Congress has not passed a federal law addressing junk e-mail, many states have passed or considered such legislation. According to the SpamLaws Web site [http://www.spamlaws.com], 27 states have passed laws regulating spam: Arkansas, California, Colorado, Connecticut, Delaware, Idaho, Illinois, Iowa, Kansas, Louisiana, Maryland, Minnesota, Missouri, Nevada, North Carolina, Oklahoma, Ohio, Pennsylvania, Rhode Island, South Dakota, Tennessee, Utah, Virginia, Washington, West Virginia, Wisconsin, and Wyoming. The specifics of each law varies. Summaries of and links to each law are provided on that Web site.

Congressional Action: 105th-107th Congresses

Congress has been debating legislation to restrict UCE for several years.[3] In the 105th Congress, the House and Senate each passed legislation (H.R. 3888, and S. 1618), but no bill ultimately cleared Congress. In the 106th Congress, several UCE bills were introduced. One, H.R. 3113 Wilson), passed the House. There was no further action. Several spam bills were introduced in the 107th Congress, but none passed. One, H.R. 718 (Wilson), was reported from the House Energy and Commerce Committee (H.Rept. 107-41, Part I), and the House Judiciary Committee (H.Rept. 107-41, Part II). The two versions were substantially different. A Senate bill, S. 630 (Burns), was reported (S.Rept. 107-318) from the Senate Commerce Committee. There was no further action.

Congressional Action: 108th Congress

S. 877 (Burns). Senators Burns introduced S. 877, the CAN SPAM Act, on April 10, 2003. It is very similar to legislation he introduced in the 107th Congress (S. 630). The bill would amend Chapter 63 of Title 18 U.S.C. (concerning mail fraud), and would:

- define UCE as commercial e-mail sent without the recipient's prior affirmative or implied consent and that is not a transactional or relationship message.

- prohibit initiating the transmission of UCE to a protected computer in the United States with knowledge and intent that the message contains or is accompanied by header information that is materially false or misleading.
- prohibit false or misleading transmission information in commercial e-mail.
- prohibit deceptive subject headings in commercial e-mail. If a person establishes and implements reasonable practices and procedures to prevent a violation of this provision, and the violation occurs despite good faith efforts to comply with them, that person would not be in violation of this provision.
- require the inclusion of a functioning return address or other Internet-based mechanism in UCE to which the recipient can opt-out. If a recipient opts-out, it would be unlawful for the sender, or a person acting on behalf of the sender, to send additional UCE more than 10 business days after receipt of the opt-out request. UCE messages would have to provide in a clear and conspicuous manner: identification that the message is an advertisement or solicitation; notice of the opportunity to opt-out; and a valid physical postal address for the sender. If a person establishes and implements reasonable practices and procedures to prevent violations, and the violation occurs despite good faith efforts to comply with them, the person would not be in violation of these provisions.
- impose statutory damages of $10 per violation (as defined in the Act) up to $500,000, or $1.5 million if the court finds that the defendant committed the violation willfully and knowingly (except that the limits do not apply to the section prohibiting false or misleading header information).
- be enforced by the FTC under the FTC Act, except for certain entities that are regulated by other agencies (e.g, national banks and federal branches and federal agencies of foreign banks would be enforced by the Office of the Comptroller of the Currency under the Federal Deposit Insurance Act).
- allow states to bring civil actions on behalf on residents of that state to enjoin practices prohibited by the Act or to obtain damages equal to the greater of actual monetary loss or statutory damages. State attorneys general would have to notify the FTC or other appropriate federal regulator and that regulator could intervene. If the FTC or another federal agency institutes a civil or administrative action for

violation of the Act, no state attorney general could bring an action against that defendant while the action was pending.

- allow an ISP that is adversely affected by a violation of the Act to bring civil action in U.S. district court to enjoin further violations or recover damages.
- supersede state or local government statutes, regulations or rules regulating the use of e-mail to send commercial messages, with exceptions.
- prohibit transmission of unlawful UCE from improperly harvested e-mail addresses.
- not impair the enforcement of sections 223 or 231 of the Communications Act of 1934, chapter 71 of Title 18 U.S.C., or any other federal criminal statute. Nothing in the Act affects the FTC's authority to bring enforcement actions regarding false or deceptive representations in commercial e-mail messages.
- not affect the lawfulness or unlawfulness under any other provision of law of the adoption, implementation, or enforcement by an ISP of a policy declining to transmit, route, relay, handle, or store certain types of e-mail.
- require the FTC to submit a study to Congress within 24 months of enactment analyzing the effectiveness and enforcement of the provisions of the Act and the need, if any, to modify those provisions.

S. 563 (Dayton). S. 563, the Computer Owners' Bill of Rights Act, includes a section that would require the FTC to establish a "do not e-mail" registry for anyone who does not wish to receive UCE, and prohibits UCE from being sent to any computer so registered unless authorized by FTC regulations.

REFERENCES

[1] The origin of the term spam for unsolicited commercial e-mail was recounted in *Computerworld*, April 5, 1999, p. 70: "It all started in early Internet chat rooms and interactive fantasy games where someone repeating the same sentence or comment was said to be making a 'spam.' The term referred to a Monty Python's Flying Circus scene in which actors keep saying 'Spam, Spam, Spam and Spam' when reading options from a menu."

[2] For more on Internet privacy issues, see CRS Report RL31408.

[3] Legislation is also pending concerning spam sent to mobile handsets, such as cellular telephones or personal digital assistants (PDAs). See CRS Report RL31636.

In: Spam and Internet Privacy
Editor: B.G. Kutais, pp. 39-56
ISBN: 978-1-59454-577-1
© 2007 Nova Science Publishers, Inc.

Chapter 3

WIRELESS PRIVACY AND SPAM: ISSUES FOR CONGRESS[*]

Marcia S. Smith

SUMMARY

Wireless communications devices such as cell phones and personal digital assistants (PDAs) are ubiquitous. Some consumers, already deluged with unwanted commercial messages, or "spam," via computers that access the Internet by traditional wireline connections, are concerned that such unsolicited advertising is expanding to wireless communications, further eroding their privacy.

In particular, federal requirements under the Enhanced 911 (E911) initiative to ensure that mobile telephone users can obtain emergency services as easily as users of wireline telephones, are driving wireless telecommunications carriers to implement technologies that can locate a caller with significant precision. Wireless telecommunications carriers then will have the ability to track a user's location any time a wireless telephone, for example, is activated. Therefore some worry that information on an individual's daily habits — such as eating, working, and shopping — will become a commodity for sale to advertising companies. As consumers walk or drive past restaurants and other businesses, they may receive calls advertising sales or otherwise soliciting their patronage. While some may

---

[*] Excerpted from CRS Report RL31636, Updated December 22, 2004

40 Marcia S. Smith

find this helpful, others may find it a nuisance, particularly if they incur usage charges.

As with the parallel debates over Internet privacy and spam, the wireless privacy discussion focuses on whether industry can be relied upon to self-regulate, or if legislation is needed. Three laws already address wireless privacy and spam concerns. The 1991 Telephone Consumer Protection Act (TCPA, P.L. 102-243) prohibits the use of autodialers or prerecorded voice messages to call wireless devices if the recipient would be charged for the call, unless the recipient has given prior consent. The 1999 Wireless Communications and Public Safety Act (the "911 Act," P.L. 106-81) expanded on privacy protections for Customer Proprietary Network Information (CPNI) held by telecommunications carriers by adding "location" to the definition of CPNI, and set forth circumstances under which that information could be used with or without the customer's express prior consent. The 2003 Controlling the Assault of Non-Solicited Pornography and Marketing Act (the CAN-SPAM Act, P.L. 108-187) required the Federal Communications Commission (FCC) to issue rules to protect wireless subscribers from unwanted mobile service commercial messages (they were issued in August 2004). Consumers also may list their cell phone numbers on the National Do Not Call Registry (there is no deadline for doing so).

Congress continues to debate how to protect wireless subscribers further. Several bills were considered in the 108th Congress. H.R. 71 would have required wireless telecommunications carriers to adhere to the fair information practices of notice, choice, and security in obtaining the express prior consent required by the 911 Act. H.R. 3558, S. 1963 and S. 1973 would have allowed wireless subscribers to choose to keep their wireless phone numbers unlisted, for free, if a wireless directory assistance database ("wireless 411") is created. S. 1963 was reported from the Senate Commerce Committee (S.Rept. 108-423). There was no legislative action on the other bills. This report is updated as warranted.

INTRODUCTION

Wireless communications devices — including mobile telephones, personal digital assistants (PDAs), pagers, and automobile-based services such as OnStar —are ubiquitous.[1] Many of the services provided by these devices require data on the user's location, whether it is to connect a phone call or dispatch emergency services when an airbag deploys.

Consumers and privacy rights advocates are increasingly concerned about the privacy implications of these wireless location-based services. If a company providing a wireless service knows the user's location, with whom can that data be shared? How long can the data be retained? Will the data be used to create individual profiles that will be sold to marketing companies or used for other purposes unknown to the user or contrary to his or her preference? Will consumers be deluged with messages on their communications devices advertising sales at nearby stores or restaurants not unlike the "spam"[2] in their e-mail inboxes?

The precision with which wireless service providers can determine a subscriber's exact location is improving with the implementation of Enhanced 911 (E911) capabilities for mobile telephones and other wireless devices, wherein wireless carriers are required to provide Public Safety Answering Points (PSAPs) with the location of wireless callers who dial 911 within 50-300 meters (150-900 feet).[3] While this serves the laudable goal of ensuring mobile telephone users immediate access to emergency services, many worry about what other uses will be made of such location information. Once the technical ability exists to provide a user's precise coordinates, some privacy advocates worry that more and more devices will incorporate it, making location information widely available without proper privacy safeguards.

The debate over wireless privacy in many ways parallels the debate over Internet privacy [4] and Internet spam. Indeed, since wireless Internet access devices are on the market, the issues intersect. One particular similarity is that the policy debate focuses on whether legislation is needed, or if industry can be relied upon to self-regulate.

Three laws address some of the issues — the Telephone Consumer Protection Act, the Wireless Communications and Public Safety Act, and the CAN-SPAM Act. Four bills were considered by the 108th Congress that further addressed wireless privacy issues, but none passed.

CONCERNS OF CONSUMERS AND PRIVACY RIGHTS ADVOCATES

Spam

Some consumers and privacy rights groups, including the Center for Democracy and Technology (CDT) [http://www.cdt.org] and the Electronic Privacy Information Center (EPIC) [http://www.epic.org], worry that the ability to identify a wireless customer's location could lead to further erosion of individual privacy. Although the E911 requirements apply only to calls made from mobile telephones seeking emergency assistance, once that capability is available, many worry that such information will be collected and sold for other purposes, such as marketing. Some observers point out that wireless carriers may be motivated to sell such customer data to recoup the costs of deploying wireless E911.

Users of wireless devices such as pagers, personal digital assistants, or automobile-based services such as OnStar, might be affected along with mobile telephone customers. A major concern is that if location information is available to commercial entities, a wireless customer walking or driving along the street may be deluged with unsolicited advertisements from nearby restaurants or stores alerting them to merchandise available in their establishments. Supporters of unsolicited advertising insist that consumers benefit from directed advertisements because they are more likely to offer products in which the consumer is interested. They also argue that advertising is protected by the First Amendment.

One aspect of this concern is that companies could build profiles of consumers using data collected over a period of time. In that context, one question is whether limits should be set on the length of time location information can be retained. Some argue that once a 911 call has been completed, or after a subscriber to a location-based service received the desired information (such as directions to the nearest restaurant), that the location information should be deleted.

Wireless spam was addressed by Congress in the CAN-SPAM Act (discussed below), although it does not focus specifically on the location aspects of the issue.

"Wireless 411" Directories

Another aspect of the wireless privacy debate concerns the rights of subscribers to have, or not have, their numbers listed in a "wireless 411" cell phone directory. Such a directory does not currently exist, but the Cellular Telecommunications & Internet Association (CTIA) is developing one for six of the seven largest mobile service providers: Alltel, Cingular, AT&T Wireless, Nextel, Sprint, and T-Mobile. (The seventh, Verizon Wireless, decided not to participate, as discussed below.) One estimate is that a wireless directory could generate as much as $3 billion a year for the wireless industry by 2009 in fees and additional minutes.[5] Qsent is the "aggregator" for the directory service.[6]

A key difference between wireless and wireline phones is that subscribers must pay for incoming as well as outgoing calls. Thus, some argue that subscribers need to be assured that they will not receive unwanted calls, not only because of a nuisance factor, but for cost reasons. Consumers may list their cell phone numbers on the National Do Not Call Registry (see CRS Report RL31642), but concerns persist about unwanted calls from telemarketers or others. (In December 2004, an e-mail was widely circulated on the Internet warning consumers that they must list their cell phone numbers on the Do Not Call list before the end of 2004, but that is incorrect. Phone numbers may be added to the Do Not Call list at any time. See [http://www. ftc.gov/donotcall/] for information on the Do Not Call list).

Questions that are arising include whether subscribers should be able to decline to have their numbers published without paying a fee (as wireline customers must do if they want an unlisted number). Proponents of the directory insist that customers will have to consent to having their numbers listed. Opponents counter that many subscribers do not realize that they already have given consent through the contract they sign with their service provider.[7] Other critics point out that wireless subscribers pay for every call, and view their cell phones as distinctly private. One of the largest mobile service providers, Verizon Wireless, decided not to participate in the directory. The company's President and CEO, Denny Strigl, argues against the notion of an "opt-in" directory, where subscribers would have to give their express prior authorization to being listed, saying that "Customers see opt-in as a disingenuous foot-in-the-door — leading to 'opt-out' clauses and fees for not publishing a number. Nor does opt-in allow customers any degree of control over how and to whom their information is revealed — they either keep full privacy or face full exposure, with nothing in-between."[8] ("Opt-in" and "Opt-out" are explained below.) Consumers Union established a website [http://www.escapecellhell.org] to encourage individuals to contact their Members of Congress in support of wireless directory legislation.

Three bills concerning wireless directories were introduced in the 108th Congress (see **108th Congress Legislation**, below). In September 2004, hearings were held by the Senate Commerce, Science, and Transportation Committee, and by the House Energy and Commerce Committee's Subcommittee on Telecommunications and the Internet. At the Senate hearing, CTIA testified that there is no need for legislation because the directory does not yet exist so it is premature to pass legislation now, the wireless industry has a proven track record in protecting consumer privacy, and subscribers would not be forced to participate in the directory nor charged a fee for opting-out. Mr. Strigl from Verizon Wireless repeated his strong opposition to the directory, but agreed that legislation is not necessary. Some opponents of the legislation point to Verizon's decision not to participate in the directory as indicative of a market-based solution to the problem, since subscribers wishing not to be listed could switch to Verizon.

Advocates of the legislation at the House hearing countered that, for example, the wireless industry's track record is less than perfect. According to *Communications Daily*,[9] Representative Pitts, sponsor of H.R. 3558, stated that when he first discussed a wireless directory with industry representatives two years ago, they insisted that opt-in was impossible, and they would need to charge for the service. Yet now, the industry is asserting that the system would be opt-in and free. Representative Markey commented that the fact that the carriers informed consumers that their numbers might become listed in a wireless directory only in the fine print of their service contracts made some observers suspicious of their intentions. Senator Boxer testified at the House hearing, noting that cell phones are quite different from home phones because people take them wherever they go, so unwanted calls are even more intrusive. She emphasized the need to allow parents to control whether their children's numbers are listed, and the need to act quickly, before the directory comes into existence. Witnesses from EPIC and the AARP testified in favor of the legislation at the Senate hearing.

Other Concerns

Other wireless privacy concerns exist, but are outside the scope of this report to discuss in depth. Briefly, some are concerned about whether law enforcement authorities might require wireless carriers to provide location information.[10] CDT's James Dempsey notes that government access to data stored on a third party network is not subject to Fourth Amendment protections that require probable cause before conducting searches.[11] CDT's Alan Davidson was quoted in *Computerworld* about other ominous implications. "'The first time somebody steals location information on the whereabouts of a kid and he goes missing, there will be a backlash and lawsuits,' he added. Or a phone company employee could have a crush on a woman with a cell phone and use the purloined data to follow her around, he said."[12]

It should be noted, however, that privacy concerns in the Internet arena, at least, often are tempered by consumers' desires for new services and low prices. The extent to which consumers would choose one wireless carrier over another purely because one promised better privacy safeguards is unclear.

FAIR INFORMATION PRACTICES

Much of the wireless privacy controversy parallels the debate over Internet privacy (see CRS Report RL31408) and spam (see CRS Report RL31953). In that context, questions have arisen over whether wireless carriers should be required to follow "fair information practices" with regard to collection, use, or dissemination of call location information.

The Federal Trade Commission (FTC) has identified four "fair information practices" for operators of commercial websites: providing *notice* to users of their information practices before collecting personal information, allowing users *choice* as to whether and how personal information is used, allowing users *access* to data collected and the ability to contest its accuracy, and ensuring *security* of the information from unauthorized use. *Enforcement* is sometimes included as a fifth practice. "Choice" is often described as "opt-in" or "opt-out." To opt-in, consumers must give their affirmative consent to a website's information practices. To opt-out, consumers are assumed to have given consent unless they indicate otherwise.

Some argue that similar practices should be observed by wireless carriers or providers of location-based information and services. A major issue is whether Congress should pass a law requiring them to do so, or if industry self-regulation is sufficient.

INDUSTRY EFFORTS TO RESPOND TO PRIVACY CONCERNS

Several industry segments are involved in the wireless privacy debate: the wireless carriers required by the FCC to provide E911 capabilities; companies offering location-based information and services; and websites that can be accessed over wireless devices.

The optimism surrounding the business potential of wireless devices is exemplified by the emergence of the terms M-Commerce (mobile

commerce) and L-Commerce (location commerce) and the creation of
industry associations to promote them. The Wireless Location Industry
Association [http://www.wliaonline.org] has developed draft wireless
privacy policy standards for its members, available on the WLIA website at
[http://www.wliaonline.org/indstandard/privacy.html]. The Mobile
Marketing Association developed a code of conduct, which is posted on its
website [http://www.mmaglobal.com/conduct/coc.html], and was adopted by
MMA's Board of Directors in November 2003. Both WLIA and MMA
combine opt-in and opt-out approaches. MMA has established a wireless
anti-spam committee in what it calls the second phase of its efforts to ensure
wireless applications are spam-free (the release of the Code of Conduct was
the first phase).

TRUSTe, a company that offers privacy "seals" to websites that follow
certain privacy guidelines, released what it called the "first wireless privacy
standards" on February 18, 2004 [http://truste.org/pdf/TRUSTe_
Wireless_Privacy_Principles.pdf]. The "Wireless Privacy and Principles and
Implementation Guidelines" call for —

- wireless service providers to give notice to their customers prior to
  or during the collection of personally identifiable information (PII),
  or upon first use of a service;
- wireless service providers to disclose customers' PII to third parties
  only if the customer has opted-in, and the customer should be able
  to change that preference at any time; and
- wireless service providers may only use location information for
  services other than those related to placing or receiving calls if the
  customer has opted-in, and wireless service providers should
  disclose the fact that they retain location information beyond the
  time reasonably needed to provide the requested service.

As part of the announcement, TRUSTe noted that it had formed a
"Wireless Advisory Committee" that includes MMA and WLIA, as well as
AT&T Wireless, Microsoft, HP, PricewaterhouseCoopers, the Center for
Democracy and Technology, and the Privacy Rights Clearinghouse. The
committee's function is "to promote privacy standards to increase consumer
use of advanced wireless features and applications." The MMA's Code of
Conduct includes a requirement to "align" with the TRUSTe principles.

The FTC held a workshop on wireless Web privacy issues in December
2000.[13] According to a media account, participants conceded that many
companies developing wireless applications are too busy implementing their

services to focus on privacy issues, and that since these companies are not certain of what future applications may emerge, "they tend to collect far more data than they need right now ... and even more collection is likely once there's ready buyer [sic] for information."[14] Some participants noted the importance of determining privacy requirements early in the development of wireless and location-based services so systems and equipment need not be retrofitted in the future.

In November 2000, CTIA asked the FCC to initiate a rulemaking, separate from its rulemaking on Customer Proprietary Network Information (CPNI, see discussion of the 911 Act, below), on implementation of the wireless location information amendments made by P.L. 106-81. CTIA argued that location privacy information is uniquely a wireless concern, and such an FCC rulemaking would attract commenters who would not be interested in the general CPNI rulemaking. CTIA asked that the FCC adopt privacy principles to assure that mobile services users would be informed of the location information collection and use practices of their service providers before the information is disclosed or used. Specifically, CTIA wanted the FCC to adopt technology neutral (i.e., for either handset- or network-based systems) rules requiring notice, choice, and "security and integrity." The latter phrase was described as meaning that location information should be protected from unauthorized use and disclosure to third parties, and third parties must adhere to the provider's location information practices. The FCC issued a Public Notice on March 16, 2001 requesting comments on CTIA's request.[15] After receiving comments and deliberating on the request, the FCC announced in July 2002 that it would not commence such a proceeding. The FCC concluded that the "statute imposes clear legal obligations and protections for consumers" and "we do not wish to artificially constrain the still-developing market for location-based services..."[16] The FCC added that it would closely monitor the issues and initiate a rulemaking proceeding "only when the need to do so has been clearly demonstrated."

EXISTING LAWS

The Telephone Consumer Protection Act (TCPA)

The 1991 Telephone Consumer Protection Act (TCPA, P.L. 102-243), *inter alia*, prohibits the use of autodialers or prerecorded voice messages to call cellular phones, pagers, or other services for which the person would be charged for the call, unless the person has given prior consent. In 2003, the FCC ruled that TCPA applies to any call that uses an automatic dialing system or artificial or recorded message to a wireless phone number, including both voice messages and text messages such as Short Message Service (SMS).[17]

In 2004, the FCC sought comment through a Notice of Proposed Rulemaking (NPRM) on two issues related to rules associated with TCPA (FCC CG Docket No. 02-278). Specifically, the NRPM addressed changes that might be necessitated by the advent of wireless Local Number Portability (LNP), which allows consumers to transfer ("port") telephone numbers they use for wireline services to wireless service providers.[18] TCPA prohibits telemarketers from placing autodialed or prerecorded calls to wireless devices, but the ability of consumers to change a "wired" number to a wireless device complicates compliance. Telemarketers complained that they could not update their call lists instantaneously, and hence did not have a reasonable opportunity to comply with the rules. In the NPRM, the FCC sought comment on whether it should institute a limited "safe harbor" for telemarketers that call telephone numbers that recently have been ported.

The Wireless Communications and Public Safety Act (the "911 Act")

Since 1996, the FCC has issued a series of orders to ensure that users of wireless phones and certain other mobile devices can reach emergency services personnel by dialing the numbers 911. The FCC rules, referred to as "Enhanced 911" or E911, apply to all cellular and Personal Communications Services (PCS) licensees, and to certain Specialized Mobile Radio licensees. A fact sheet describing the FCC's actions is available at [http://www.fcc.gov/911/enhanced]. This report addresses only the privacy implications of the availability of the call location information that will enable wireless E911 to work. Other E911 issues, including implementation, are discussed in CRS Report RS21028 and CRS Report RS21222.

Because the technologies needed to implement E911 will enable wireless telecommunications carriers to track, with considerable precision,[19] a user's location any time the device is activated, some worry that information on an individual's daily habits — such as eating, working, and shopping — will become a commodity for sale to advertising companies, for example.

In 1999, Congress passed the Wireless Communications and Public Safety Act (P.L. 106-81), often called "the 911 Act." In addition to making 911 the universal emergency assistance number in the United States, the 911 Act also amended section 222 of the Communications Act of 1934 (47 U.S.C. §222), which establishes privacy protections for **customer proprietary network information (CPNI)** held by telecommunications carriers. *Inter alia*, the 911 Act added "location" to the definition of CPNI.

Under section 222(h), as amended, CPNI is defined as:

> (A) information that relates to the quantity, technical configuration, type, destination, location, and amount of use of a telecommunications service subscribed to by any customer of a telecommunications carrier, and that is made available to the carrier by the customer solely by virtue of the carrier-customer relationship; and (b) information contained in the bills pertaining to telephone exchange service or telephone toll service received by a customer of a carrier, except that such term does not include subscriber list information.

Section 222 required the FCC to establish rules regarding how telecommunications carriers treat CPNI. The FCC adopted its Third Report and Order on CPNI on July 16, 2002,[20] setting forth a dual approach in which "opt-in" is required in some circumstances, and "opt-out" is permitted in others.[21]

In addition to adding location to the definition of CPNI, the 911 Act amended section 222(d)(4) regarding authorized uses of CPNI. As amended, the law determines those circumstances under which wireless carriers need to obtain a customer's prior consent to use wireless location information, and when prior consent is not required. A customer's prior consent is *not* required (section 222 (d)) —

- to provide call location information to a PSAP or to emergency service and law enforcement officials in order to respond to the user's call for emergency services;
- to inform the user's legal guardian or members of the user's immediate family of the user's location in an emergency situation that involves the risk of death or serious physical harm; or
- to information or database management services providers solely for purposes of assistance in the delivery of emergency services in response to an emergency.

In a newly created section 222(f), the 911 Act states that, except in the circumstances listed above, *without express prior authorization*, customers shall not be considered to have approved the use or disclosure of or access to (1) call location information, or (2) automatic crash notification information to anyone other than for use in an automatic crash notification system.

The phrase "express prior authorization" is not further defined in the law, however, nor the measures telecommunications carriers must take to obtain it. H.R. 71 (see **108th Congress Legislation**, below) would have set such requirements.

The CAN-SPAM Act

In 2003, Congress passed a broad anti-spam bill, the CAN-SPAM Act (P.L. 108-187), which is addressed in more detail in CRS Report RL31953. The original version of the bill, S. 877, and the version passed by the Senate on October 22, 2003, did not address spam on wireless devices. The House, however, added such a provision (Sec. 14) in the version it passed on November 21, 2003. The Senate amended several provisions of S. 877, including the section on wireless spam, when it concurred with the House version on November 25, 2003. The House adopted the Senate version on December 8. The bill was signed into law by President Bush on December 16, 2003.

The law required the FCC, in consultation with the FTC, to promulgate rules within 270 days of enactment to protect consumers from unwanted **"mobile service commercial messages"** (**MSCMs**). That term is defined in the law as a commercial e-mail message "that is transmitted directly to a wireless device that is utilized by a subscriber of commercial mobile service" as defined in the 1934 Communications Act. (In this report, an MSCM is referred to as a wireless commercial e-mail message.)

The FCC announced a Notice of Proposed Rulemaking on March 11, 2004. According to *Communications Daily*,[22] during the comment period, several wireless carriers and the CTIA urged that they be exempted from the requirement to obtain express prior authorization before sending commercial messages to their customers if the customers are not charged for them, arguing that those are carrier-customer relationship issues and are protected by the First Amendment. CTIA reportedly agreed with the FCC's preliminary interpretation[23] that the CAN-SPAM Act applies only to messages sent to an e-mail address consisting of two parts, a unique user name or mailbox and a reference to an Internet domain (e.g.

janedoe@wirelesscarrier.com), and therefore should not apply to SMS, short code or other text messages sent using other address formats.

The FCC adopted the new rules on August 4, 2004; they were released on August 12.[24] Most went into effect on October 18, 2004, although several that deal with information collection requirements must obtain approval of the Office of Management and Budget. The FCC took the following actions:

- Prohibited sending wireless commercial e-mail messages unless the individual addressee has given the sender express prior authorization ("opt-in"), which may be given orally or in writing, including electronically. Requests for such authorization may not be sent to a wireless subscriber's wireless device because of the potential costs to the subscriber for receiving, accessing, reviewing and discarding such mail. Authorization provided to a particular sender does not entitle that sender to send wireless commercial e-mail messages on behalf of third parties, including affiliated entities and marketing partners. The request for authorization must contain specified information, such as the fact that the recipient may be charged by their wireless service provider for receiving the message, and subscribers may revoke their authorization at any time.

The rules do not apply to —

messages that are forwarded by a subscriber to his or her own wireless device (although they do apply to any person who receives consideration or inducement to forward the message to someone else's wireless device), or

phone-to-phone SMS messages if they are not autodialed (Internet-to-phone SMS messages *are* covered by the rules since they involve a domain name address).

- Announced that it would create a publicly available FCC wireless domain names list with the domain names used for mobile service messaging so that senders of commercial mail can determine which addresses are directed at mobile services, and —

Prohibited sending any commercial message to addresses that have been on the list for at least 30 days, or at any time prior to 30 days if the sender otherwise knows that the message is addressed to a wireless device, and

Required all wireless service providers to supply the FCC with the names of all Internet domains on which they offer mobile service messaging services.

- Determined that all autodialed calls, including SMS, are already covered by the TCPA.
- Interpreted the definition of wireless commercial e-mail message to include any commercial message sent to an e-mail address provided by a wireless service provider (formally called a "commercial mobile radio service," or CMRS) specifically for delivery to the subscriber's wireless device.
- Provided guidance on the definition of "commercial," but noted that the Federal Trade Commission is ultimately responsible for determining the criteria for "commercial" and "transactional or relationship" messages.

As noted, some wireless service providers sought an exemption from the requirement to obtain express prior authorization for them to communicate with their own subscribers, as long as the subscribers did not incur additional costs. The FCC did not grant such as exemption, in part because it concluded that the existing exemption in the CAN-SPAM Act for transactional or relationship messages is sufficient to cover many types of communication needed between a provider and a subscriber. Furthermore, the Commission concluded that the CAN-SPAM Act required it to protect consumers from unwanted commercial messages, not only those that involve additional costs.

108TH CONGRESS LEGISLATION

As discussed above, the 108th Congress passed, and the President signed into law, the CAN-SPAM Act (P.L. 108-187) which includes provisions related to wireless spam. Four other bills were introduced: H.R. 71 (Frelinghuysen), H.R. 3558 (Pitts), S. 1963 (Specter) and S. 1973 (DeWine). None of these cleared Congress.

Wireless Privacy: H.R. 71 (Frelinghuysen)

H.R. 71 would have amended the Wireless Communications and Public Safety Act to require that wireless carriers provide notice, choice, and security. It stated that a customer would not be considered to have granted express prior authorization unless the carrier provided the customer, in writing, a clear, conspicuous, and complete disclosure of the carrier's practices regarding collection and use of location information, transaction information, and automatic crash identification information, before any such information is disclosed or used. The disclosure would have had to include a description of the specific types of information collected by the carriers, how the carrier uses such information, and what information might be shared or sold to other companies and third parties. The customer would have had to agree in writing to the collection and use of such information, or agree to its collection and use subject to certain limitations. The carriers would have had to establish and maintain procedures to protect the confidentiality, security, and integrity of the information. The FCC would have been responsible for developing regulations to implement these amendments. The bill was referred to the House Energy and Commerce Committee. There was no further action.

"Wireless 411" Directory Assistance: H.R. 3558 (Pitts), S. 1963 (Specter), and S. 1973 (DeWine)

H.R. 3558, S. 1963 and S. 1973 were virtually identical bills, each entitled "Wireless 411 Privacy Act." The bills would have enabled wireless subscribers to choose to keep their wireless telephone numbers unlisted, for free, if a directory assistance database for wireless subscribers is created. CTIA, is assembling such a database (discussed above).[25] The legislation would have required commercial mobile service providers to obtain express prior authorization ("opt-in") from each current or new subscriber, separate from any authorization obtained to provide the subscriber with mobile service, to include the subscriber's wireless phone number in that database. Call forwarding from a directory assistance operator to a subscriber would have been permitted only if the operator first informed the subscriber of who was calling and the subscriber could accept or reject the incoming call on a per-call basis, and the subscriber's phone number would not have been disclosed to the calling party. Call forwarding would not have been permitted to subscribers whose numbers were unlisted. The bills would also have prohibited commercial mobile service providers from publishing, in print, electronic, or other form, the contents of any wireless directory assistance database. No fees could have been charged to subscribers for keeping their phone numbers private. H.R. 3558 was referred to the House Energy and Commerce Committee, and S. 1963 and S. 1973 to the Senate Commerce, Science, and Transportation Committee.

The Senate Commerce Committee held a hearing on S. 1963 on September 21, 2004. The bill was marked up the next day. After considerable debate, and adoption of a Boxer substitute amendment, the bill was ordered reported (12-10). A written report was filed on December 7, 2004 (S.Rept. 108-423). There was no further action in the Senate.

The House Energy and Commerce Committee held a hearing on this topic on September 29, 2004. The hearings are discussed above (see **"Wireless 411" Directories**). There was no further action in the House.

REFERENCES

[1] The Cellular Telecommunications & Internet Association (CTIA) maintains a counter on its website [http://www.ctia.org] showing the number of U.S. wireless subscribers. On November 1, 2004, the figure was approximately 171 million.

[2] For more information on "spam," see CRS Report RL31953, *"Spam": An Overview of Issues Concerning Commercial Electronic Mail*, by Marcia S. Smith.

[3] For more information on E911, see CRS Report RS21222, *Implementing Wireless Enhanced 911 (E911): Issues for Public Safety Answering Points (PSAPs)*, by Linda K. Moore, and CRS Report RS21028, *Wireless Enhanced 911 (E911): Issues Update*, by Linda K. Moore.

[4] For more on Internet privacy, see CRS Report RL31408: *Internet Privacy: Overview and Pending Legislation*, by Marcia S. Smith.

[5] Shiver, Jube Jr. Coming Soon: a Cellphone Directory. Los Angeles Times, May 20, 2004, p. A1 (via Factiva), citing a study by the Zelos Group Inc.

[6] See [http://www.qsent.com/news/news-2004-09-21-1.shtml].

[7] At a Senate Commerce Committee hearing on September 21, 2004, Kathleen Pierz of The Pierz Group testified that nearly all mobile subscribers, except Cingular Wireless customers, have already signed a

contract that includes their express permission to have their mobile number listed in any type of directory the carrier chooses.

[8]   Verizon Wireless CEO Calls for Preserving Customer Privacy and Open Competition at Yankee Group Wireless Summit. Verizon Wireless Press Release, June 21, 2004. [http://news.vzw.com/news/2004/06/pr2004-06-21.html]

[9]   Carriers Promise Congress Wireless 411 Will Protect Privacy. Communications Daily, September 30, 2004, p. 2.

[10] Some of these concerns stem from the Communications Assistance for Law Enforcement Act (CALEA). See CRS Report RL30677, *Digital Surveillance: the Communications Assistance for Law Enforcement Act*, by Patricia Moloney Figliola.

[11] Quoted in: Communications Daily, June 20, 2001, p. 3.

[12] Quoted in: Computerworld, October 2, 2000, p. 10

[13] The transcript of the FTC's two-day (Dec. 11-12, 2000) workshop is available in two parts (day 1 and day 2) at [http://www.ftc.gov/bcp/workshops/wireless/001211.htm] and [http://www.ftc.gov/bcp/workshops/wireless/001212.htm].

[14] Communications Daily, December 13, 2000, p. 4. At the time, CTIA stood for Cellular Telecommunications Industry Association. The organization later changed its name to Cellular Telecommunications & Internet Association, and now is referred to as CTIA — the Wireless Association [http://www.ctia.org].

[15] Federal Communications Commission. Wireless Telecommunications Bureau Seeks Comment on Request to Commence Rulemaking to Establish Fair Location Information Practices. WT Docket No. 01-72. March 16, 2001. DA 01-696.

[16] Federal Communications Commission. Order. WT Docket No. 01-72. FCC 02-208. Adopted July 8, 2002; released July 24, 2002.

[17] SMS is generally defined as a short (less than 160 alpha-numeric characters) message that contains no text or graphics.

[18] For more on Local Number Portability, see CRS Report RL30052, *Telephone Bills: Charges on Local Telephone Bills*, by James R. Riehl, or the FCC's website: [http://www.fcc.gov/cgb/NumberPortability].

[19] Under Phase 2 of E911 implementation, wireless carriers are required to provide "Automatic Location Identification" (ALI) information to PSAPs that will locate the caller's latitude and longitude within 50-300 meters (150-900 feet), depending on the technology used. (If handset-based technology is used, the caller's location must be identified within 50 meters for 67% of calls; within 150 meters for 95% of calls. If

network-based technology is used, the location must be identified within 100 meters for 67% of the calls; within 300 meters for 95% of calls.)

[20] Federal Communications Commission. Third Report and Order and Third Further Notice of Proposed Rulemaking. CC Docket No. 96-115. Adopted July 16, 2002; Released July 25, 2002.

[21] Opt-in means that an individual's affirmative consent is required. Opt-out means that consent is assumed unless the individual indicates otherwise. A full discussion on the FCC's CPNI rules is outside the scope of this report. See the aforementioned FCC third report and order for further information.

[22] Wireless Industry Asks for Exemption From Seeking Opt-In Consent. Communications Daily, May 4, 2004, p. 4.

[23] See paragraph 10 of the FCC's NPRM.

[24] Federal Communications Commission. FCC Takes Action to Protect Wireless Subscribers from Spam. Press Release, August 4, 2004. [http://hraunfoss.fcc.gov/edocs_public/attachmatch/DOC-250522A3.pdf]. The rules were released on August 14, 2004, and are available at the website of the FCC's Office of Consumer and Governmental Affairs [http://www.fcc.gov/cgb/]. CG Docket No. 04-53 and CG Docket No. 02-278.

[25] Shiver, Jube. Coming Soon: A Cellphone Directory. Los Angeles Times, May 20, 2004, A-1 (via Factiva).

In: Spam and Internet Privacy
Editor: B.G. Kutais, pp. 57-86

Chapter 4

INTERNET PRIVACY: OVERVIEW AND PENDING LEGISLATION*

Marcia S. Smith

SUMMARY

Internet privacy issues generally encompass two types of concerns. One is the collection of personally identifiable information (PII) by website operators from visitors to government and commercial websites, or by software that is surreptitiously installed on a user's computer ("spyware") and transmits the information to someone else. The other is the monitoring of electronic mail and Web usage by the government or law enforcement officials, employers, or Internet Service Providers.

The September 11, 2001 terrorist attacks intensified debate over the issue of law enforcement monitoring, with some advocating increased tools for law enforcement to track down terrorists, and others cautioning that fundamental tenets of democracy, such as privacy, not be endangered in that pursuit. Congress passed the 2001 USA PATRIOT Act (P.L. 107-56) that, *inter alia*, makes it easier for law enforcement to monitor Internet activities. That act was later amended by the Homeland Security Act (P.L. 107-296), loosening restrictions as to when, and to whom, Internet Service Providers can voluntarily release information about subscribers if they believe there is a danger of death or injury. Privacy advocates are monitoring how the act is

---

* Excerpted from CRS Report RL31408, Updated July 6, 2004

implemented. Legislation is pending regarding whether to add, or remove, "sunset" provisions for certain sections of the act.

The debate over website information policies concerns whether industry self regulation or legislation is the best approach to protecting consumer privacy. Congress has considered legislation that would require *commercial* website operators to follow certain fair information practices, but none has passed. Legislation has passed, however, regarding information practices for *federal government* websites e.g, the E-Government Act (P.L. 107-347). Meanwhile, controversy is rising about how to protect computer users from spyware without creating unintended consequences. Spyware is not well defined, but generally includes software emplaced on a computer without the user's knowledge that takes control of the computer away from the user, such as by redirecting the computer to unintended websites, causing advertisements to appear, or collecting information and transmitting it to another person. Four spyware bills are pending; one (H.R. 2929) has been ordered reported from committee.

Identity theft is not an Internet privacy issue, but is often debated in the context of whether the Internet makes identity theft more prevalent. Thus, it is briefly discussed in this report. For more information on that topic, see CRS Report RL31919, *Remedies Available to Victims of Identity Theft*, and CRS Report RL32121, *Fair Credit Reporting Act: A Side-by-Side Comparison of House, Senate and Conference Versions.*

This report provides an overview of Internet privacy, tracks Internet privacy legislation pending before the 108th Congress, and describes the laws that were enacted in the 107th Congress. For information on wireless privacy issues, see CRS Report RL31636, *Wireless Privacy: Availability of Location Information for Telemarketing.* This report will be updated.

INTRODUCTION

Internet privacy issues encompass concerns about the collection of personally identifiable information (PII) from visitors to government and commercial websites, as well as debate over law enforcement or employer monitoring of electronic mail and Web usage. This report discusses Internet privacy issues and tracks pending legislation. More information on Internet privacy issues is available in CRS Report RL30784, *Internet Privacy: An Analysis of Technology and Policy Issues*, and CRS Report RL31289, *The Internet and the USA PATRIOT Act: Potential Implications for Electronic Privacy, Security, Commerce, and Government.*

INTERNET: COMMERCIAL WEBSITE PRACTICES

One aspect of the Internet ("online") privacy debate focuses on whether industry self regulation or legislation is the best route to assure consumer privacy protection. In particular, consumers appear concerned about the extent to which website operators collect "personally identifiable information" (PII) and share that data with third parties without their knowledge. Repeated media stories about privacy violations by website operators have kept the issue in the forefront of public debate about the Internet. Although many in Congress and the Clinton Administration preferred industry self regulation, the 105th Congress passed legislation (COPPA, see below) to protect the privacy of children under 13 as they use commercial websites. Many bills have been introduced since that time regarding protection of those not covered by COPPA, but the only legislation that has passed concerns federal government, not commercial, websites.

Children's Online Privacy Protection Act (COPPA), P.L. 105-277

Congress, the Clinton Administration, and the Federal Trade Commission (FTC) initially focused their attention on protecting the privacy of children under 13 as they visit commercial websites. Not only are there concerns about information children might divulge about themselves, but also about their parents. The result was the Children's Online Privacy Protection Act (COPPA), Title XIII of Division C of the FY1999 Omnibus Consolidated and Emergency Supplemental Appropriations Act, P.L. 105-277. The FTC's final rule implementing the law became effective April 21, 2000 [http://www.ftc.gov/os/1999/10/64fr59888.htm]. Commercial websites and online services directed to children under 13, or that knowingly collect information from them, must inform parents of their information practices and obtain verifiable parental consent before collecting, using, or disclosing personal information from children. The law also provides for industry groups or others to develop self-regulatory "safe harbor" guidelines that, if approved by the FTC, can be used by websites to comply with the law. The FTC approved self-regulatory guidelines proposed by the Better Business Bureau on January 26, 2001. FTC Chairman Muris stated in testimony to the Senate Commerce Committee on June 11, 2003 that the FTC had brought eight COPPA cases, and obtained agreements requiring payment of civil penalties totaling more than $350,000.[1]

FTC Activities and Fair Information Practices

The FTC has conducted or sponsored several website surveys since 1997 to determine the extent to which commercial website operators abide by four fair information practices—providing **notice** to users of their information practices before collecting personal information, allowing users **choice** as to whether and how personal information is used, allowing users **access** to data collected and the ability to contest its accuracy, and ensuring **security** of the information from unauthorized use.   Some include **enforcement** as a fifth fair information practice. Regarding choice, the term **"opt-in"** refers to a requirement that a consumer give affirmative consent to an information practice, while **"opt-out"** means that permission is assumed unless the consumer indicates otherwise.   See CRS Report RL30784 for more information on the FTC surveys and fair information practices. The FTC's reports are available on its website [http://www.ftc.gov].

Briefly, the first two FTC surveys (December 1997 and June 1998) created concern about the information practices of websites directed at children and led to the enactment of COPPA (see above).   The FTC continued monitoring websites to determine if legislation was needed for those not covered by COPPA.   In 1999, the FTC concluded that more legislation was not needed at that time because of indications of progress by industry at self-regulation, including creation of "seal" programs (see below) and by two surveys conducted by Georgetown University. However, in May 2000, the FTC changed its mind following another survey that found only 20% of randomly visited websites and 42% of the 100 most popular websites had implemented all four fair information practices. The FTC voted to recommend that Congress pass legislation requiring websites to adhere to the four fair information practices, but the 3-2 vote indicated division within the Commission. On October 4, 2001, FTC's new chairman, Timothy Muris, revealed his position on the issue, saying that he did not see a need for additional legislation now.

Advocates of Self Regulation

In 1998, members of the online industry formed the Online Privacy Alliance (OPA) to encourage industry self regulation. OPA developed a set of privacy guidelines, and its members are required to adopt and implement posted privacy policies. The Better Business Bureau (BBB), TRUSTe, and WebTrust have established "seals" for websites. To display a seal from one of those organizations, a website operator must agree to abide by certain privacy principles (some of which are based on the OPA guidelines), a complaint resolution process, and to being monitored for compliance. Advocates of self regulation argue that these seal programs demonstrate industry's ability to police itself.

Technological solutions also are being offered. P3P (Platform for Privacy Preferences) is one often-mentioned technology. It gives individuals the option to allow their web browser to match the privacy policies of websites they access with the user's selected privacy preferences. Its goal is to put privacy in the hands of the consumer. P3P is one of industry's attempts to protect privacy for online users. Josh Freed from the Internet Education Foundation says there is strong private sector backing for P3P as a first step in creating a common dialogue on privacy, and support from Congress, the Administration, and the FTC as well (see the IEF website [http://www.p3ptoolbox.org/tools/papers/IEFP3POutreachforDMA.ppt]).

The CATO Institute, argues that privacy-protecting technologies are quite effective [http://www.cato.org/pubs/briefs/bp-065es.html]. However, complaints are arising from some industry participants as P3P is implemented. One concern is that P3P requires companies to produce shortened versions of their privacy policies to enable them to be machine-readable. To some, this raises issues of whether the shortened policies are legally binding, since they may omit nuances, and "sacrifice accuracy for brevity."[2]

Advocates of Legislation

Consumer, privacy rights and other interest groups believe self regulation is insufficient. They argue that the seal programs do not carry the weight of law, and that while a site may disclose its privacy policy, that does not necessarily equate to having a policy that protects privacy. The Center for Democracy and Technology (CDT, at [http://www.cdt.org]) and the Electronic Privacy Information Center (EPIC, at [http://www.epic.org]) each have released reports on this topic. TRUSTe and BBBOnline have been criticized for becoming corporate apologists rather than defenders of privacy. In the case of TRUSTe, for example, Esther Dyson, who is credited with playing a central role in the establishment of the seal program, reportedly is disappointed with it. Wired.com reported in April 2002 that "Dyson agreed that...Truste's image has slipped from consumer advocate to corporate apologist. 'The board ended up being a little too corporate, and didn't have any moral courage,' she said." Truste subsequently announced plans to strengthen its seal program by more stringent licensing requirements and increased monitoring of compliance.

Some privacy interest groups, such as EPIC, also feel that P3P is insufficient, arguing that it is too complex and confusing and fails to address many privacy issues. An EPIC report from June 2000 further explains its findings [http://www.epic.org/reports/prettypoorprivacy.html].

Privacy advocates are particularly concerned about online profiling, where companies collect data about what websites are visited by a particular user and develop profiles of that user's preferences and interests for targeted advertising. Following a one-day workshop on online profiling, FTC issued a two-part report in the summer of 2000 that also heralded the announcement by a group of companies that collect such data, the Network Advertising Initiative (NAI), of self-regulatory principles. At that time, the FTC nonetheless called on Congress to enact legislation to ensure consumer privacy vis a vis online profiling because of concern that "bad actors" and others might not follow the self-regulatory guidelines. As noted, the current FTC Chairman's position is that broad legislation is not needed at this time.

107th Congress Action

Many Internet privacy bills were considered by, but did not clear, the 107th Congress. H.R. 89, H.R. 237, H.R. 347, and S. 2201 dealt specifically with commercial website practices. H.R. 4678 was a broader consumer privacy protection bill. The Bankruptcy Reform bill (H.R. 333/S. 420) would have prohibited (with exceptions) companies, including website operators, that file for bankruptcy from selling or leasing PII obtained in accordance with a policy that said such information would not be transferred to third parties, if that policy was in effect at the time of the bankruptcy filing. H.R. 2135 would have limited the disclosure of personal information (defined as PII and sensitive personal information) by information recipients in general, and S. 1055 would have limited the commercial sale and marketing of PII. In a related measure, S. 2839 sought to protect the privacy of children using elementary or secondary school or library computers that use "Internet content management services," such as filtering software to restrict access to certain websites.

During the second session of the 107th Congress, attention focused on S. 2201 (Hollings) and H.R. 4678 (Stearns). (H.R. 4678 has been reintroduced in the 108th Congress, see below.) A fundamental difference was that H.R.

4678 affected privacy for both "online" and "offline" data collection entities, while S. 2201's focus was online privacy. During markup by the Senate Commerce Committee, a section was added to S. 2201 directing the FTC to issue recommendations and propose regulations regarding entities other than those that are online. Other amendments also were adopted. The bill was reported on August 1, 2002 (S.Rept. 107-240). A House Energy and Commerce subcommittee held a hearing on H.R. 4678 on September 24, 2002. There was no further action on either bill.

Legislation in the 108th Congress

Representative Frelinghuysen introduced H.R. 69 on the opening day of the 108th Congress. The bill would require the FTC to prescribe regulations to protect the privacy of personal information collected from and about individuals not covered by COPPA

Table 1. Major Provisions of H.R. 1636 (Stearns)
(Explanation of Acronyms at End)

Provision	H.R. 1636 (Stearns) As Introduced
Title	Consumer Privacy Protection Act
Entities Covered	Data Collection Organizations, defined as entities that collect (by any means, through any medium), sell, disclose for consideration, or use, PII. Excludes governmental agencies, not-for-profit entities if PII not used for commercial purposes, certain small businesses, certain providers of professional services, and data processing outsourcing entities.
Differentiation Between Sensitive and Non-Sensitive PII	No

Table 1. continued

Provision	H.R. 1636 (Stearns) As Introduced
Adherence to Fair Information Practices	
Notice	Yes, with exceptions
Choice	Yes (Opt-Out)
Access	No
Security	Yes
Enforcement	By FTC
Private Right of Action	No
Relationship to State Laws	Preempts state statutory laws, common laws, rules, or regulations, that affect collection, use, sale, disclosure, retention, or dissemination of PII in commerce.
Relationship to Other Federal Laws	Does not modify, limit, or supersede specified federal privacy laws, and compliance with relevant sections of those laws is deemed compliance with this act.
Permitted Disclosures	Consumer's choice to preclude sale, or disclosure for consideration, by an entity applies only to sale or disclosure to another data collection organization that is not an information-sharing affiliate (as defined in the act) of the entity.
Establishes Self-Regulatory "Safe Harbor"	Yes
Requires Notice to Users If Entity's Privacy Policy Changes	Yes
Requires Notice to Users if Privacy is Breached	No
Identity Theft Prevention and Remedies	Yes
Requires GAO study of impact on U.S. interstate and foreign commerce of foreign information privacy laws, and remediation by Secretary of Commerce if GAO finds discriminatory treatment of U.S. entities	Yes

Table 1. continued

Provision	H.R. 1636 (Stearns) As Introduced
Requires Secretary of Commerce to notify other nations of provisions of the act, seek recognition of its provisions, and seek harmonization with foreign information privacy laws, regulations, or agreements.	Yes

FTC = Federal Trade Commission
GAO = General Accounting Office
PII = Personally Identifiable Information

On April 3, 2003, Representative Stearns introduced H.R. 1636, which is similar to H.R. 4678 from the 107th Congress.   It addresses privacy for both online and offline entities. Its major provisions are shown in Table 1.

Senator Feinstein introduced S. 745 on March 31, 2003.   Title 1 of that bill requires commercial entities to provide notice and choice (opt-out) to individuals regarding the collection and disclosure or sale of their PII, with exceptions.   She also introduced S. 1350 on June 26, 2003, which would require federal agencies and persons engaged in interstate commerce, who possess electronic data containing personal information, to disclose any unauthorized acquisition of that data. A Senate Judiciary subcommittee held a hearing on S. 1350 in November 2003.

INTERNET: FEDERAL GOVERNMENT WEBSITE INFORMATION PRACTICES

Under a May 1998 directive from President Clinton and a June 1999 Office of Management and Budget (OMB) memorandum, federal agencies must ensure that their information practices adhere to the 1974 Privacy Act. In June 2000, however, the Clinton White House revealed that contractors for the Office of National Drug Control Policy (ONDCP) had been using "cookies" (small text files placed on users' computers when they access a particular website) to collect information about those using an ONDCP site during an anti-drug campaign.   ONDCP was directed to cease using cookies, and OMB issued another memorandum reminding agencies to post and comply with privacy policies, and detailing the limited circumstances under which agencies should collect personal information. A September 5, 2000 letter from OMB to the Department of Commerce further clarified that "persistent"cookies, which remain on a user's computer for varying lengths of time (from hours to years), are not allowed unless four specific conditions are met. "Session" cookies, which expire when the user exits the browser, are permitted.

At the time, Congress was considering whether commercial websites should be required to abide by FTC's four fair information practices. The incident sparked interest in whether federal websites should adhere to the same requirements. In the FY2001 Transportation Appropriations Act (P.L. 106-346), Congress prohibited funds in the FY2001 Treasury-Postal Appropriations Act from being used to collect, review, or create aggregate lists that include PII about an individual's access to or use of a federal website or enter into agreements with third parties to do so, with exceptions. Similar language is in the FY2002 Treasury-Postal Appropriations Act (P.L. 107-67). The FY2003 Treasury-Postal appropriations bills (sec. 634 in both H.R. 5120 and S. 2740) also contained similar language, though the bill did not clear the 107th Congress.

Section 646 of the FY2001 Treasury-Postal Appropriations Act (P.L. 106-554) required Inspectors General (IGs) to report to Congress on activities by those agencies or departments relating to their own collection of PII, or entering into agreements with third parties to obtain PII about use of websites. Then-Senator Fred Thompson released two reports in April and June 2001 based on the findings of agency IGs who discovered unauthorized persistent cookies and other violations of government privacy guidelines on several agency websites.   An April 2001 GAO report (GAO-01-424) concluded that most of the 65 sites it reviewed were following OMB's guidance.

The107th Congress passed the E-Government Act (P.L. 107-347), which sets requirements on government agencies regarding how they assure the privacy of personal information in government information systems and establish guidelines for privacy policies for federal websites.   The law requires federal websites to include a privacy notice that addresses what information is to be collected, why, its intended use, what notice or opportunities for consent are available to individuals regarding what is collected and how it is shared, how the information will be secured, and the rights of individuals under the 1974 Privacy Act and other relevant laws. It also requires federal agencies to translate their website privacy policies into a standardized machine-readable format, enabling P3P to work (see above discussion of P3P), for example. According to a February 2004 Federal

Computer Week article, agency implementation of that provision is proceeding slowly.[3]

MONITORING OF E-MAIL AND WEB USAGE

By Government and Law Enforcement Officials

Another concern is the extent to which electronic mail (e-mail) exchanges or visits to websites may be monitored by law enforcement agencies or employers. In the wake of the September 11 terrorist attacks, the debate over law enforcement monitoring has intensified. Previously, the issue had focused on the extent to which the Federal Bureau of Investigation (FBI), with legal authorization, uses a software program, called Carnivore (later renamed DCS 1000), to intercept e-mail and monitor Web activities of certain suspects. The FBI installs the software on the equipment of Internet Service Providers (ISPs). Privacy advocates are concerned whether Carnivore-like systems can differentiate between e-mail and Internet usage by a subject of an investigation and similar usage by other people. Section 305 of the 21st Century Department of Justice Appropriations Authorization Act (P.L. 107-273) required the Justice Department to report to Congress at the end of FY2002 and FY2003 on its use of Carnivore/DCS 1000 or any similar system.

On the other hand, following the terrorist attacks, Congress passed the Uniting and Strengthening America by Providing Appropriate Tools to Intercept and Obstruct Terrorism (USA PATRIOT) Act (P.L. 107-56), which expands law enforcement's ability to monitor Internet activities. *Inter alia*, the law modifies the definitions of "pen registers" and "trap and trace devices" to include devices that monitor addressing and routing information for Internet communications. Carnivore-like programs may now fit within the new definitions. The Internet privacy-related provisions of the USA PATRIOT Act, included as part of Title II, are as follows:

- Section 210, which expands the scope of subpoenas for records of electronic communications to include records commonly associated with Internet usage, such as session times and duration.
- Section 212, which allows ISPs to divulge records or other information (but not the contents of communications) pertaining to a subscriber if they believe there is immediate danger of death or serious physical injury or as otherwise authorized, and requires

them to divulge such records or information (excluding contents of communications) to a governmental entity under certain conditions. It also allows an ISP to divulge the contents of communications to a law enforcement agency if it reasonably believes that an emergency involving immediate danger of death or serious physical injury requires disclosure of the information without delay. **[This section was amended by the Homeland Security Act, see below.]**

- Section 216, which adds routing and addressing information (used in Internet communications) to dialing information, expanding what information a government agency may capture using pen registers and trap and trace devices as authorized by a court order, while excluding the content of any wire or electronic communications. The section also requires law enforcement officials to keep certain records when they use their own pen registers or trap and trace devices and to provide those records to the court that issued the order within 30 days of expiration of the order. To the extent that Carnivore-like systems fall with the new definition of pen registers or trap and trace devices provided in the act, that language would increase judicial oversight of the use of such systems.
- Section 217, which allows a person acting under color of law to intercept the wire or electronic communications of a computer trespasser transmitted to, through, or from a protected computer under certain circumstances, and
- Section 224, which sets a four-year sunset period for many of the Title II provisions. Among the sections excluded from the sunset are Sections 210 and 216.

The Cyber Security Enhancement Act, section 225 of the Homeland Security Act (P.L. 107-296), amends section 212 of the USA PATRIOT Act.[4]   It lowers the threshold for when ISPs may voluntarily divulge the content of communications. Now ISPs need only a "good faith" (instead of a "reasonable") belief that there is an emergency involving danger (instead of "immediate" danger) of death or serious physical injury. The contents can be disclosed to "a Federal, state, or local governmental entity" (instead of a "law enforcement agency").

Privacy advocates are especially concerned about the new language added by the Cyber Security Enhancement Act. EPIC notes, for example, that allowing the contents of Internet communications to be disclosed voluntarily to any governmental entity not only poses increased risk to personal privacy, but also is a poor security strategy. Another concern is that the law does not provide for judicial oversight of the use of these procedures.[5]

S. 1695 (Leahy) would amend the PATRIOT Act to provide more oversight. *Inter alia,* it would amend the sunset provision (Sec. 224) such that all of the above cited sections would terminate on December 31, 2005, including Sections 210 and 216, which currently are not subject to the sunset clause. S. 1709 (Craig) would amend the USA PATRIOT Act, *inter alia,* to include Sec. 216 in the sunset clause. By contrast, S. 2476 (Kyl), would repeal Sec. 224 so that none of the provisions sunset.

By Employers

There also is concern about the extent to which employers monitor the e-mail and other computer activities of employees. The public policy concern appears to be not whether companies should be able to monitor activity, but whether they should notify their employees of that monitoring. A 2003 survey by the American Management Association [http://www.amanet.org/research/index.htm] found that 52% of the companies surveyed engage in some form of e-mail monitoring. A September 2002 General Accounting Office report (GAO-02-717) found that, of the 14 Fortune 1,000 companies it surveyed, all had computer-use policies, and all stored employee's electronic transactions, e-mail, information on websites visited, and computer file activity. Eight of the companies said they would read and review those transactions if they received other information than an individual might have violated company policies, and six said they routinely analyze employee's transactions to find possible inappropriate uses.

By E-Mail Service Providers

In what is widely-regarded as a landmark ruling concerning Internet privacy, the U.S. Court of Appeals for the First Circuit in Massachusetts ruled (2-1) on June 29, 2004 that an e-mail service provider did not violate federal wiretapping statutes when it intercepted and read subscribers' e-mails to obtain a competitive business advantage. The ruling upheld the decision of a lower court to dismiss the case.

The case involved an e-mail service provider, Interloc, Inc., that sold out-of-print books. According to press accounts[6] and the text of the court's ruling,[7] Interloc used software code to intercept and copy e-mail messages sent to its subscribers (who were dealers looking for buyers of rare and out-of-print books) by competitor Amazon.com.   The e-mail was intercepted and copied prior to its delivery to the recipient so that Interloc officials could read the e-mails and obtain a competitive advantage over Amazon.com.   Interloc Vice President Bradford Councilman was charged with violating the Wiretap Act.[8,9] The court's majority opinion noted that the parties stipulated that, at all times that the Interloc software was performing operations on the e-mails, they existed in the random access memory or in hard drives within Interloc's computer system.

The case turned on the distinction between the e-mail being in transit, or in storage (and therefore governed by a different law[10]). The government argued that the e-mails were copied contemporaneously with their transmission, and therefore were intercepted under the meaning of the Wiretap Act. Judges Torruella and Cyr concluded, however, that they were in temporary storage in Interloc's computer system, and therefore were not subject to the provisions of the Wiretap Act. They further stated that "We believe that the language of the statute makes clear that Congress meant to give lesser protection to electronic communications than wire and oral communication. Moreover, at this juncture, much of the protection may have been eviscerated by the realities of modern technology.... However, it is not the province of this court to graft meaning onto the statute where Congress has spoken plainly." (p. 14-15). In his dissent, Judge Lipez stated, conversely, that he did not believe Congress intended for e-mail that is temporarily stored as part of the transmission process to have less privacy than messages as they are in transit.   He agreed with the government's contention that an "intercept" occurs between the time the author hits the "send" button and the message arrives in the recipient's in-box. He concluded that "Councilman's approach to the Wiretap Act would undo decades of practice and precedent ... and would essentially render the act irrelevant .... Since I find it inconceivable that Congress could have intended such a result merely by omitting the term 'electronic storage' from its definition of 'electronic communication,' I respectfully dissent."[11]

Privacy advocates expressed deep concern about the ruling. Electronic Frontier Foundation (EFF) attorney Kevin Bankston stated that the court had "effectively given Internet communications providers free rein to invade the privacy of their users for any reason and at any time."[12] The five major ISPs (AOL, Earthlink, Microsoft, Comcast, and Yahoo) all reportedly have policies governing their terms of service that state that they do not read subscribers' e-mail or disclose personal information unless required to do so by law enforcement agencies.[13]

SPYWARE

What is Spyware?

The term "spyware" is not well defined. Jerry Berman, President of the Center for Democracy and Technology (CDT), explained in testimony to the Senate Commerce Committee in March 2004 that "The term has been applied to software ranging from 'keystroke loggers' that capture every key typed on a particular computer; to advertising applications that track users' web browsing; to programs that hijack users' system settings."[14] He noted that what these various types of software programs "have in common is a lack of transparency and an absence of respect for users' ability to control their own computers and Internet connections." The FTC held a workshop on spyware on April 19, 2004.

One example of spyware is software products that include, as part of the software itself, a method by which information is collected about the use of the computer on which the software is installed. Some products may collect personally identifiable information (PII). When the computer is connected to the Internet, the software periodically relays the information back to the software manufacturer or a marketing company. Some spyware traces a user's Web activity and causes advertisements to suddenly appear on the user's monitor — called "pop-up" ads —in response. Software programs that include spyware can be sold or provided for free, on a disk (or other media) or downloaded from the Internet. Typically, users have no knowledge that spyware is on their computers.

As noted, spyware also can refer to "keylogging" software that records a person's keystrokes. All typed information thus can be obtained by another party, even if the author modifies or deletes what was written, or if the characters do not appear on the monitor (such as when entering a password). Commercial key logging software has been available for some time, but its existence was highlighted in 2001 when the FBI, with a search warrant, installed the software on a suspect's computer, allowing them to obtain his password for an encryption program he used, and thereby evidence. Some privacy advocates argue wiretapping authority should have been obtained, but the judge, after reviewing classified information about how the software works, ruled in favor of the FBI. Press reports also indicate that the FBI is developing a "Magic Lantern" program that performs a similar task, but can be installed on a subject's computer remotely by surreptitiously including it in an e-mail message, for example. Privacy advocates question what type of legal authorization should be required.

108th Congress Spyware Legislation

Four spyware bills are pending before the 108th Congress, of which one, H.R. 2929, has been acted upon in committee.

H.R. 2929 (Bono) was ordered reported from the House Energy and Commerce Committee on June 24, 2004, after adoption of a substitute version offered by Representative Stearns. The text of the Stearns substitute, called **the SPY ACT** (Securely Protect Yourself Against Cyber Trespass Act), is available at [http://energycommerce.house.gov/108/Markups/06242004/ains_fc_xml.pdf]). As ordered reported, the act, which would expire on December 31, 2009, includes the following provisions.

Section 2, which would become effective on the date the law is enacted, prohibits deceptive acts or practices relating to spyware. It would be unlawful for anyone who is not the owner or authorized user (hereafter, the user) of a protected computer to —

→ take control of the computer by utilizing the computer to send unsolicited information or material from the computer to others, diverting the computer's browser away from the site the user intended to view, accessing or using the computer's Internet connection and thereby damaging the computer or causing the user to incur unauthorized financial charges, using the computer as part of an activity performed by a group of computers that causes damage to another computer, or delivering advertisements that a user cannot close without turning off the computer or closing all sessions of the Internet browser;

→ modify settings related to use of the computer or the computer's access to the Internet by altering the Web page that appears when the browser is launched, the default provider used to access or search the Internet, the list of bookmarks, or security or other settings that protect information about the user;

→ collect personally identifiable information through keylogging;

→ induce the user to install software, or prevent reasonable efforts to block the installation or execution of, or to disable, software, by presenting the user with an option to decline installation but the installation nevertheless proceeds, or causing software that has been properly removed or disabled to automatically reinstall or reactivate;

→   misrepresent that certain actions or information is needed to open, view, or play a particular type of content;

→   misrepresent the identity or authority of a person or entity providing software in order to induce the user to install or execute the software;

→   misrepresent the identity or authority of a person seeking information in order to induce the user to provide personally identifiable information (this practice is commonly called "phishing");

→   remove, disable, or render inoperative security, anti-spyware, or anti-virus technology installed on the computer;

→   install or execute on the computer one or more additional software components with the intent of causing a person to use such component in a way that violates any other provision of this section.

Section 3 prohibits the collection of certain information without notice and consent. It contains an opt-in requirement, wherein it would be unlawful for anyone to transmit any information collection program, or execute any information collection functions installed on a computer, without obtaining consent from the user before the information collection program is executed for the first time. "Information collection program" is defined as software the collects personally identifiable information and sends it to a person other than the user, or uses such information to deliver or display advertising; or collects information regarding Web pages accessed using the computer and uses such information to deliver or display advertising. The bill specifies certain requirements for notice (differentiating among various types of software at issue) and consent. If multiple collection programs first execute any of the information collection functions of the programs together, only one notice is required. However, the user must be notified and consent obtained if the information collected or sent is materially changed.   Users must be able to disable or remove the information collection program without undue effort or knowledge. Telecommunications carriers, information service or interactive computer service providers, cable operators, or providers of transmission capability are not liable under the act. Section 3 would become effective one year after the law is enacted, and would not apply to information collection programs installed on a computer prior to that date.

The Federal Trade Commission is directed to enforce the act, and is either directed or permitted to promulgate rules for various sections. Civil penalties are set for various violations. Exceptions are made for a variety of law enforcement/national security-related activities, and for network providers that use monitoring software to protect network security and prevent fraud. The act would supersede state laws that expressly regulate deceptive conduct similar to that described in the act, or the transmission or execution of a computer program similar to that described in the act, or the use of context-based triggering mechanisms or similar means to display advertisements. It would not preempt other state trespass, contract, or tort laws, or other state laws to the extent they relate to fraud.

The Stearns substitute reportedly responded to industry concerns about earlier versions of the legislation, but some Members and lobbyists continue to express reservations, and further changes are possible before the bill reaches the House floor.[15]

Three other bills are pending.

- H.R. 4255 (Inslee), the Computer Software Privacy and Control Act, requires notice to and consent of a user before anyone installs software on a user's computer (not including pre-installed software, and certain other exceptions) that collects certain information about the owner or operator of the computer and transmits it to anyone other than the owner or operator; that modifies the operation of the computer without the consent of the owner or operator and without including a removal utility; or that delivers or displays advertisements without the consent of the owner or operator and without including a removal utility. Referred to the House Energy & Commerce and House Judiciary Committees.

- H.R. 4661 (Goodlatte), the I-SPY Prevention Act, creates criminal penalties for certain spyware practices: up to five-years in prison for anyone using software to intentionally break into a computer and use the software in furtherance of another federal crimes; and up to two years in prison for anyone using software to intentionally break into a computer and then altering the computer's security settings or obtaining personal information with the intent to defraud or injure a person, or with the intent to damage a computer. Referred to the House Judiciary Committee.

- S. 2145 (Burns-Wyden), the SPY BLOCK (Software Principles Yielding Better Levels of Consumer Knowledge) Act, requires notice to and consent of a user before anyone installs software on a user's computer (not including pre-installed software, and certain other exceptions). It also requires the user's affirmative consent to each information collection feature, advertising feature, distributed computing feature, and setting modification feature in the software. The software also must be able to be easily uninstalled. Referred to the Commerce, Science, and Transportation Committee; hearing held March 23, 2004.

Arguments For and Against Legislation

The Senate Commerce Committee's Communications Subcommittee held a hearing on S. 2145 on March 23, 2004. Witnesses discussed the difficulties in legislating in an area where definitions are unclear, and the pace of technology might quickly render any such definitions obsolete. Mr. Robert Holleyman, representing the Business Software Alliance, testified that the focus of legislation should be regulating bad behavior, not technology. He expressed reservations about S. 2145, and called on Congress not to preclude the evolution of tools and marketplace solutions to the problem. Mr. John L. Levine, author of *The Internet for Dummies* and similar books, concluded that the legislation should ban spyware banned entirely, or consumers should be able to give a one-time permanent notice (akin to the telemarketing Do Not Call list) that they do not want spyware on their computers. He also said that the legislation should allow consumers to sue violators, rather than relying only on the FTC and state Attorneys General to enforce the law. Mr. Berman of CDT noted that three existing laws (including the FTC Act) can be used to address spyware concerns, and that technology measures, self-regulation and user education also are important to dealing with spyware. He concluded that CDT believes that new legislation specifically targeted at spyware would be useful, but that Congress also should pass broad Internet privacy legislation that could address the privacy aspects of the spyware debate.

While there is concern generally about any software product installed without the user's knowledge or consent, one particular area of controversy is programs that cause pop-up ads to appear. Many users object to pop-up ads as vigorously as they do to unsolicited commercial e-mail ("spam" — see CRS Report RL31953). The extent to which pop-up ads are, or should be, included in a definition of spyware was discussed at the Senate Commerce Committee hearing. Mr Avi Naider, President and CEO of WhenU.com, argued that although his company's WhenU software does create pop-up ads, it is not spyware because users are notified that the program is about to be installed, must affirmatively consent to a license agreement, and may decline it. Mr. Naider explained that his program often is "bundled" with software that users obtain for free (called "free-ware"), or a software developer may offer users a choice between paying for the software or obtaining it for free if they agree to receive ads from WhenU. While agreeing that spyware is a serious concern, and that Congress and the FTC should regulate in this area, Mr. Naider urged that legislation be written carefully to exclude products like his that offer notice and choice and therefore should not be considered spyware. As noted below, WhenU has filed suit against a Utah law regulating spyware.

The House Energy and Commerce's Subcommittee on Telecommunications and the Internet held a hearing on April 29, 2004. At the hearing, FTC representatives argued that many of the actions under the rubric of "spyware" already are illegal, and additional legislation is not needed and could have unintended consequences because of the difficulty in defining spyware. A CDT witness again argued in favor of broad privacy legislation rather than focusing only on spyware. A representative from Earthlink supported legislation. A witness from Microsoft said that his company supports a "holistic" solution, but did not clearly state whether he supported new legislation or not.

Utah's Spyware Law

On March 23, 2004, the Governor of Utah signed an anti-spyware law, which became effective on May 3, 2004.[16] The definition of spyware in that law includes certain pop-up ads. It prohibits, for example, some pop-up ads that partially or wholly cover or obscure paid advertising or other content on a website in a way that interferes with a user's ability to view the website. A media report stated that passage of the law was "driven by a Utah company in a legal fight with a pop-up company."[17] The Utah law also defines spyware, inter alia, as software installed on a computer without the user's consent and that cannot be easily disabled and removed. Several high-tech companies reportedly argued that the law could have unintended consequences, for example, prohibiting parents from installing software to block access by their children to certain Websites because the software monitors Web activities, may have been installed without the child's consent, and the child may not be able to uninstall it easily.[18]

WhenU filed suit against the Utah law on constitutional grounds, and Utah legislators reportedly are considering modifications to the law.[19] The Third Judicial District Court in Salt Lake City, Utah granted a preliminary injunction on June 22, 2004, preventing the law from taking effect.[20] As noted above, H.R. 2929 would supersede state spyware laws.

IDENTITY THEFT

Identity theft is not an Internet privacy issue, but the perception that the Internet makes identity theft easier means that it is often discussed in the Internet privacy context.   The concern is that the widespread use of computers for storing and transmitting information is contributing to the rising rates of identity theft, where one individual assumes the identity of another using personal information such as credit card and Social Security numbers (SSNs). The FTC has a toll free number (877-ID-THEFT) to help victims.[21]

Whether the Internet is responsible for the increase in cases is debatable. Some attribute the rise instead to carelessness by businesses in handling personally identifiable information, and by credit issuers that grant credit without proper checks. In a 2003 survey for the FTC, Synovate found that 51% of victims do not know how their personal information was obtained by the thief; 14% said their information was obtained from lost or stolen wallets, checkbooks, or credit cards;13% said the personal information was obtained during a transaction; 4% cited stolen mail; and 14% said the thief used "other" means (e.g. the information was misused by someone who had access to it such as a family member or workplace associate).[22]

Several laws have been passed regarding identity theft (P.L. 105-318, P.L. 106-433, and P.L. 106-578), but Congress continues to assess ways to reduce the incidence of identity theft and help victims.

On December 4, 2003, the President signed the most recent law, the Fair and Accurate Credit Transactions Act (H.R. 2622, P.L. 108-159). It is discussed in detail in CRS Report RL32121, *Fair Credit Reporting Act: A Side-By-Side Comparison of House, Senate, and Conference Versions.* Among its identity theft-related provisions, the law —

- requires consumer reporting agencies to follow certain procedures concerning when to place, and what to do in response to, fraud alerts on consumers' credit files;
- allows consumers one free copy of their consumer report each year from nationwide consumer reporting agencies as long as the consumer requests it through a centralized source under rules to be established by the FTC;[23]
- allows consumers one free copy of their consumer report each year from nationwide specialty consumer reporting agencies (medical records or payments, residential or tenant history, check writing history, employment history, and insurance claims) upon request pursuant to regulations to be established by the FTC; [14]
- requires credit card issuers to follow certain procedures if additional cards are requested within 30 days of a change of address notification for the same account;
- requires the truncation of credit card numbers on electronically printed receipts;
- requires business entities to provide records evidencing transactions alleged to be the result of identity theft to the victim and to law enforcement agencies authorized by the victim to take receipt of the records in question;
- requires consumer reporting agencies to block the reporting of information in a consumer's file that resulted from identity theft and to notify the furnisher of the information in question that it may be the result of identity theft;
- requires federal banking agencies, the FTC, and the National Credit Union Administration to jointly develop guidelines for use by financial institutions, creditors and other users of consumer reports regarding identity theft;
- extends the statute of limitations for when identity theft cases can be brought; and
- allows consumers to request that the first five digits of their Social Security Numbers not be included on a credit report provided to the consumer by a consumer reporting agency.

A number of other bills have been introduced in the 108th Congress regarding identity theft and protection of Social Security Numbers. They are described in Table 2 below. One, H.R. 1731, has passed the House and Senate. It makes aggravated identity theft in conjunction with felonies a crime, and establishes mandatory sentences — 2 additional years beyond the penalty for the underlying crime, or 5 additional years for those who steal identities in conjunction with a terrorist act.[24]

SUMMARY OF PENDING 108TH CONGRESS LEGISLATION

The following table summarizes legislation pending before the 108th Congress concerning Internet privacy and identity theft (including protection of Social Security Numbers).

Table 2. Pending Internet Privacy-Related Legislation

INTERNET PRIVACY (GENERAL)	
Bill	**Summary/Committee of Referral**
H.R. 69 Frelinghuysen	**Online Privacy Protection Act.** Requires the FTC to prescribe regulations to protect the privacy of personal information collected from and about individuals not covered by COPPA. (Energy & Commerce)
H.R. 1636 Stearns	**Consumer Privacy Protection Act.** See Table 1 for summary of provisions. (Energy & Commerce)
S. 745 Feinstein	**Privacy Act.** Title I requires commercial entities to provide notice and choice (opt-out) to individuals regarding the collection and disclosure or sale of their PII, with exceptions. (Judiciary)
S. 1350 Feinstein	**Notification of Risk to Personal Data.** Requires federal agencies and persons engaged in interstate commerce, who possess electronic data containing personal information, to disclose any unauthorized acquisition of that data. (Judiciary)
S. 1695 Leahy	**PATRIOT Oversight Restoration Act.** *Inter alia*, would sunset Sections 210 and 216 of the USA PATRIOT Act on Dec. 31, 2005 (those sections are not subject to the sunset provisions now included in the act). (Judiciary)
S. 1709 Craig	**Security and Freedom Ensured (SAFE) Act.** *Inter alia* would sunset Section 216 of the USA PATRIOT Act on December 31, 2005. (Judiciary)
S. 2476 Kyl	[no title]. Would repeal section 224 of the USA PATRIOT Act, which sunsets certain provisions of that law. (Judiciary)

Table 2. continued

Bill	Summary/Committee of Referral
	SPYWARE
H.R. 2929 Bono **Ordered reported from committee**	**Safeguard Against Privacy Invasions Act.** Requires the FTC to establish regulations prohibiting the transmission of spyware programs via the Internet to computers without the user's consent, and notification to the user that the program will be used to collect personally identifiable information (PII). **Ordered reported from Energy & Commerce Committee June 24, 2004.**
H.R. 4255 Inslee	**Computer Software Privacy and Control Act.** To prevent deceptive software transmission practices. (Energy & Commerce; Judiciary)
H.R. 4661 Goodlatte	**I-SPY Prevention Act.** Sets criminal penalties for certain spyware practices. (Judiciary)
S. 2145 Burns	**SPY BLOCK** (Software Principles Yielding Better Levels of Consumer Knowledge). To regulate the authorized installation of computer software, and to require clear disclosure to computer users of certain computer software features that may pose a threat to user privacy. (Commerce) Hearing held March 23, 2004.
	IDENTITY THEFT/SOCIAL SECURITY NUMBER PROTECTION
H.R. 70 Frelinghuysen	**Social Security On-Line Privacy Protection Act.** Regulates the use by interactive computer services of Social Security numbers (SSNs) and related personally identifiable information (PII). (Energy & Commerce)
H.R. 220 Paul	**Identity Theft Protection Act.** Protects the integrity and confidentiality of SSNs, prohibits establishment of a uniform national identifying number by federal government, and prohibits federal agencies from imposing standards for identification of individuals on other agencies or persons. (Ways & Means; Government Reform)
H.R. 637 Sweeney	**Social Security Misuse Prevention Act.** Limits the display, sale, or purchase of SSNs. H.R. 637 referred to House Ways & Means
S. 228 Feinstein	Committee. S. 228 placed on Senate calendar. [The Senate bill was reintroduced from the 107th Congress, where it was reported from the Senate Judiciary Committee on May 16, 2002—no written report. The bill number in that Congress was S. 848.]

Table 2. continued

Bill	Summary/Committee of Referral
H.R. 818 Kleczka	**Identity Theft Consumers Notification Act.** Requires financial institutions to notify consumers whose personal information has been compromised. (Financial Services)
H.R. 858 Tanner	**Identity Theft Penalty Enhancement Act.** Increases penalties for aggravated identity theft. (Judiciary)
H.R. 1729 Carson	**Negative Credit Information Act.** Requires consumer reporting agencies to notify consumers if information adverse to their interests is added to their files. (Financial Services)
H.R. 1731 Carter **Passed House and Senate**	**Identity Theft Penalty Enhancement Act.** Establishes penalties for aggravated identity theft. Passed House June 23; Senate June 25. Cleared for the White House June 25.
H.R. 1931 Kleczka	**Personal Information Privacy Act.** Protects SSNs and other personal information through amendments to the Fair Credit Reporting Act. (Ways & Means, Financial Services)
H.R. 2035 Hooley	**Identity Theft and Financial Privacy Protection Act.** Requires credit card issuers to confirm change of address requests if received within 30 days of request for additional card; requires consumer reporting agencies to include a fraud alert in a consumer's file if the consumer has been, or suspects he or she is about to become, a victim of identity theft; requires truncation of credit and debit card numbers on receipts; requires FTC to set rules on complaint referral, investigations, and inquiries. (Financial Services)
H.R. 2617 Shadegg	**Consumer Identity and Information Security Act.** Prohibits the display of SSNs, with exceptions, and restricts the use of SSNs; prohibits the denial of products or services because an individual will not disclose his or her SSN; requires truncation of credit and debit card numbers on receipts; requires card issuers to verify a consumer's identity if a request for an additional credit card is made, or for a debit card or any codes or other means of access associated with it; requires FTC to set up a centralized reporting system for consumers to report suspected violations. (Financial Services, Ways & Means, Energy & Commerce)

Table 2. continued

Bill	Summary/Committee of Referral
H.R. 2633 Emmanuel	**Identity Theft Protection and Information Blackout Act.** Restricts the sale of SSNs and prohibits the display of SSNs by governmental agencies; prohibits the display, sale or purchase of SSNs in the private sector, with exceptions; and makes refusal to do business with anyone who will not provide an SSN an unfair or deceptive act or practice under the FTC Act, with exceptions. (Ways & Means, Energy & Commerce, Judiciary, Financial Services)
H.R. 2971 Shaw	**Social Security Number Privacy and Identity Theft Protection Act.** Restricts the sale of SSNs and prohibits the display of SSNs by governmental agencies; prohibits the display, sale or purchase of SSNs in the private sector, with exceptions; makes refusal to do business with anyone who will not provide an SSN an unfair or deceptive act or practice under the FTC Act; and requires certain methods of verification of identity when issuing or replacing SSNs and cards. (Ways & Means, Financial Services, Energy & Commerce)
H.R. 3233 Gutierrez	**Identity Theft Notification and Credit Restoration Act.** Requires financial institutions and financial services providers to notify customers of the authorized use of personal information, amends the Fair Credit Reporting Act to require fraud alerts to be included in consumer credit files, and provides consumers with enhanced access to credit reports in such cases. (Financial Services)
H.R. 3693 Scott	**Identity Theft Investigation and Prosecution Act.** Provides additional resources to the Department of Justice for investigating and prosecuting identity theft and related credit card and other fraud. (Judiciary)
S. 153 Feinstein **Passed Senate**	**Identity Theft Penalty Enhancement Act.** Increases penalties for identity theft. (Judiciary) [This bill was reintroduced from the 107th Congress where it was reported by the Senate Judiciary Committee on November 14, 2002—no written report. The bill number in that Congress was S. 2541.] **Passed Senate without amendment March 19, 2003.**

Table 2. continued

Bill	Summary/Committee of Referral
S. 223 Feinstein	**Identity Theft Prevention Act.** Requires credit card numbers to be truncated on receipts; imposes fines on credit issuers who issue new credit to identity thieves despite the presence of a fraud alert on the consumer's credit file; entitles each consumer to one free credit report per year from the national credit bureaus; and requires credit card companies to notify consumers when an additional credit card is requested on an existing credit account within 30 days of an address change request. (Banking)
S. 745 Feinstein	**Privacy Act.** Title II is the Social Security Misuse Prevention Act (S. 228, see above H.R. 637/S. 228 above).
S. 1533 Cantwell	**Identity Theft Victims Assistance Act.** Requires business entities with knowledge of an identity theft to share information with the victim or law enforcement agencies and requires consumer reporting agencies to block dissemination of information resulting from an identity theft, with exceptions. This bill is reintroduced from the 107th Congress where it was S 1742. (Judiciary)
S. 1581 Cantwell	**Identity Theft Victims Assistance Act.** Similar to S. 1533, but *inter alia* expressly states that the bill does not provide for private right of action, establishes an affirmative defense, and excludes consumer reporting agencies that are reselling information from some of the act's provisions under specified conditions. (Judiciary)
S. 1633 Corzine	**Identity Theft and Credit Restoration Act.** Requires financial institutions and financial service providers to notify customers of the unauthorized use of personal information, requires fraud alerts to be included in consumer credit files in such cases, and provides customers with enhanced access to credit reports in such cases. (Banking)
S. 1749 Specter	**Prevent Identity Theft From Affecting Lives and Livelihoods (PITFALL) Act.** Amends the Consumer Protection Act to provide relief for victims of identity theft. (Banking)

APPENDIX: INTERNET PRIVACY-RELATED LEGISLATION PASSED BY THE 107TH CONGRESS

H.R. 2458 (Turner)/ **S. 803** (Lieberman) **P.L. 107-347**	**E-Government Act**. *Inter alia*, sets requirements on government agencies in how they assure the privacy of personal information in government information systems and establish guidelines for privacy policies for federal websites.
H.R. 5505 (Armey) **P.L. 107-296**	**Homeland Security Act**. Incorporates **H.R. 3482, Cyber Security Enhancement Act**, as Sec. 225. Loosens restrictions on ISPs, set in the USA PATRIOT Act, as to when, and to whom, they can voluntarily release information about subscribers.
H.R. 2215 (Sensenbrenner) **P.L. 107-273**	**21st Century Department of Justice Authorization Act**. Requires the Justice Department to notify Congress about its use of Carnivore (DCS 1000) or similar Internet monitoring systems.
H.R. 3162 (Sensenbrenner) **P.L. 107-56**	**USA PATRIOT Act**. Expands law enforcement's authority to monitor Internet activities. See CRS Report RL31289 for how the act affects use of the Internet. Amended by the Homeland Security Act (see P.L. 107-296).

REFERENCES

[1] Prepared statement, p. 10, available at [http://commerce.senate.gov/hearings/index.cfm].

[2] Clark, Drew. Tech, Banking Firms Criticize Limitations of Privacy Standard. NationalJournal.com, November 11, 2002.

[3] Michael, Sara. Privacy Safeguard Proves Elusive. Federal Computer Week, February 23, 2004 (via Factiva).

[4] The language originated as H.R. 3482, which passed the House on June 15, 2002.

[5] [http://www.epic.org/alert/EPIC_Alert_9.23.html]. See entry under "[3] Homeland Security Bill Limits Open Government, and click on hyperlink to EPIC's February 26, 2002 letter to the House Judiciary Committee.

[6] Jewell, Mark. Interception of E-Mail Raises Questions. Associated Press, June 30, 2004, 9:14 pm. (2) Zetter, Kim. E-Mail Snooping Ruled

Permissible. Wired News, June 30, 2004, 08:40. (3) Krim, Jonathan. Court Limits Privacy of E-Mail Messages; Providers Free to Monitor Communications. Washington Post, July 1, 2004, E1 (via Factiva).

[7]   U.S. v Bradford C. Councilman. U.S. Court of Appeals for the First Circuit. No. 03-1383. [http://www.ca1.uscourts.gov/pdf.opinions/03-1383-01A.pdf].

[8]   The Wiretap Act,18 U.S.C. §§ 2510-2522, is Title I of the Electronic Communications Privacy Act (ECPA), P.L. 99-508.

[9]   According to Jewell, op. cit., two other defendants—Alibris, which bought Interloc in 1998, and Interloc's systems administrator—pleaded guilty.

[10] Stored communications are covered by the Stored Communications Act, which is Title II of ECPA, 18 U.S.C. §§ 2701-2711.

[11] U.S. v Bradford C. Councilman, p. 53.

[12] Online Privacy "Eviscerated" by First Circuit Decision. June 29, 2004. [http://www.eff.org/news/archives/2004_06.php#001658].

[13] Krim, op. cit.

[14] Testimony to the Senate Committee on Commerce, Science, and Transportation, Subcommittee on Communications, March 23, 2004. Available on CDT's spyware site [http://www.cdt.org/privacy/spyware/] along with a November 2003 CDT report entitled Ghosts in Our Machines: Background and Policy Proposals on the "Spyware" Problem.

[15] 'Spyware' Regulation Bill Approved. CQ Weekly, June 25, 2004, p. 1564. (2) House Commerce Clears Spyware Bill; Some Feel It's Rushed. Warren's Washington Internet Daily, June 25, 2004 (via Factiva); (3) McCullagh, Declan. Anti-Spyware Bill Heads for House. C|NET News.com, June 24, 2004, 12:24 pm PDT.

[16] See [http://www.le.state.ut.us/~2004/bills/hbillenr/hb0323.pdf] for the enrolled text of the law.

[17] Tech Companies Lobby Utah Governor Against Broad Anti-Spyware Bill. Warren's Washington Internet Daily, March 22, 2004 (via Factiva).

[18] Utah Anti-Spyware Bill Opposed by High-Tech Becomes Law. Warren's Washington Internet Daily, March 25, 2004 (via Factiva).

[19] Wallace, Brice. Deseret Morning News, April 22, 2004, E01 (via Factiva).

[20] Judge Grants NY Pop-Up Company Preliminary Injunction Against Spyware Law. Associated Press, June 23, 2004, 06:06 (via Factiva).

[21] See also CRS Report RS21162, *Remedies Available to Victims of Identity Theft*; and CRS Report RS21083, *Identity Theft and the Fair Credit Reporting Act: an Analysis of TRW v. Andrews and Current Legislation*.

[22] Synovate. Federal Trade Commission—Identity Theft Survey Report. September 2003. P. 30-31. [http://www.ftc.gov/opa/2003/09/idtheft.htm]

[23] The FTC rules on free credit reports were issued on June 4, 2004 and are available at [http://www.ftc.gov/opa/2004/06/freeannual.htm].

[24] Senate Clears Tougher Penalties for Identity Theft in Conjunction with Felony. CQ Weekly, June 26, 2004, p. 1561.

In: Spam and Internet Privacy
Editor: B.G. Kutais, pp. 87-116
ISBN: 978-1-59454-577-1
© 2007 Nova Science Publishers, Inc.

Chapter 5

ONE HUNDRED EIGHTH CONGRESS OF THE UNITED STATES OF AMERICA AT THE FIRST SESSION

Begun and held at the City of Washington on Tuesday, the seventh day of January, two thousand and three

AN ACT

To regulate interstate commerce by imposing limitations and penalties on the transmission of unsolicited commercial electronic mail via the Internet.

Be it enacted by the Senate and House of Representatives of the United States of America in Congress assembled,

SECTION 1. SHORT TITLE

This Act may be cited as the "Controlling the Assault of Non-Solicited Pornography and Marketing Act of 2003", or the "CAN-SPAM Act of 2003".

SEC. 2. CONGRESSIONAL FINDINGS AND POLICY

(a) FINDINGS.—The Congress finds the following:

(1) Electronic mail has become an extremely important and popular means of communication, relied on by millions of Americans on a daily basis for personal and commercial purposes. Its low cost and global reach make it extremely convenient and efficient, and offer unique opportunities for the development and growth of frictionless commerce.

(2) The convenience and efficiency of electronic mail are threatened by the extremely rapid growth in the volume of unsolicited commercial electronic mail. Unsolicited commercial electronic mail is currently estimated to account for over half of all electronic mail traffic, up from an estimated 7 percent in 2001, and the volume continues to rise. Most of these messages are fraudulent or deceptive in one or more respects.

(3) The receipt of unsolicited commercial electronic mail may result in costs to recipients who cannot refuse to accept such mail and who incur costs for the storage of such mail, or for the time spent accessing, reviewing, and discarding such mail, or for both.

(4) The receipt of a large number of unwanted messages also decreases the convenience of electronic mail and creates a risk that wanted electronic mail messages, both commercial and noncommercial, will be lost, overlooked, or discarded amidst the larger volume of unwanted messages, thus reducing the reliability and usefulness of electronic mail to the recipient.

(5) Some commercial electronic mail contains material that many recipients may consider vulgar or pornographic in nature.

(6) The growth in unsolicited commercial electronic mail imposes significant monetary costs on providers of Internet access services, businesses, and educational and nonprofit institutions that carry and receive such mail, as there is a finite volume of mail that such providers, businesses,

andinstitutions can handle without further investment in infrastructure.

(7) Many senders of unsolicited commercial electronic mail purposefully disguise the source of such mail.

(8) Many senders of unsolicited commercial electronic mail purposefully include misleading information in the messages' subject lines in order to induce the recipients to view the messages.

(9) While some senders of commercial electronic mail messages provide simple and reliable ways for recipients to reject (or "opt-out" of) receipt of commercial electronic mail from such senders in the future, other senders provide no such "opt-out" mechanism, or refuse to honor the requests of recipients not to receive electronic mail from such senders in the future, or both.

(10) Many senders of bulk unsolicited commercial electronic mail use computer programs to gather large numbers of electronic mail addresses on an automated basis from Internet websites or online services where users must post their addresses in order to make full use of the website or service.

(11) Many States have enacted legislation intended to regulate or reduce unsolicited commercial electronic mail, but these statutes impose different standards and requirements. As a result, they do not appear to have been successful in addressing the problems associated with unsolicited commercial electronic mail, in part because, since an electronic mail address does not specify a geographic location, it can be extremely difficult for law-abiding businesses to know with which of these disparate statutes they are required to comply.

(12) The problems associated with the rapid growth and abuse of unsolicited commercial electronic mail cannot be solved by Federal legislation alone. The development and adoption of technological approaches and the pursuit of cooperative efforts with other countries will be necessary as well.

(b) CONGRESSIONAL DETERMINATION OF PUBLIC POLICY.—On the basis of the findings in subsection (a), the Congress determines that—

(1) there is a substantial government interest in regulation of commercial electronic mail on a nationwide basis;

(2) senders of commercial electronic mail should not mislead recipients as to the source or content of such mail; and

(3) recipients of commercial electronic mail have a right to decline to receive additional commercial electronic mail from the same source.

SEC. 3. DEFINITIONS

In this Act:

(1) AFFIRMATIVE CONSENT.—The term "affirmative consent", when used with respect to a commercial electronic mail message, means that—

(A) the recipient expressly consented to receive the message, either in response to a clear and conspicuous request for such consent or at the recipient's own initiative; and

(B) if the message is from a party other than the party to which the recipient communicated such consent, the recipient was given clear and conspicuous notice atthe time the consent was communicated that the recipient's electronic mail address could be transferred to such other party for the purpose of initiating commercial electronic mail messages.

(2) COMMERCIAL ELECTRONIC MAIL MESSAGE.—

(A) IN GENERAL.—The term "commercial electronic mail message" means any electronic mail message the primary purpose of which is the commercial advertisement or promotion of a commercial product or service (including content on an Internet website operated for a commercial purpose).

(B) TRANSACTIONAL OR RELATIONSHIP MESSAGES.—The term "commercial electronic mail message" does not include a transactional or relationship message.

(C) REGULATIONS REGARDING PRIMARY PURPOSE.—Not later than 12 months after the date of the enactment of this Act, the Commission shall issue regulations pursuant to section 13 defining the relevant criteria to facilitate the determination of the primary purpose of an electronic mail message.

(D) REFERENCE TO COMPANY OR WEBSITE.—The inclusion of a reference to a commercial entity or a link to the website of a commercial entity in an electronic mail message does not, by itself, cause such message to be treated as a commercial electronic mail message for purposes of this Act if the contents or circumstances of the message indicate a primary purpose other than commercial advertisement or promotion of a commercial product or service.

(3) COMMISSION.—The term "Commission" means the Federal Trade Commission.

(4) DOMAIN NAME.—The term "domain name" means any alphanumeric designation which is registered with or assigned by any domain name registrar, domain name registry, or other domain name registration authority as part of an electronic address on the Internet.

(5) ELECTRONIC MAIL ADDRESS.—The term "electronic mail address" means a destination, commonly expressed as a string of characters, consisting of a unique user name or mailbox (commonly referred to as the "local part") and a reference to an Internet domain (commonly referred to as the "domain part"), whether or not displayed, to which an electronic mail message can be sent or delivered.

(6) ELECTRONIC MAIL MESSAGE.—The term "electronic mail message" means a message sent to a unique electronic mail address.

(7) FTC ACT.—The term "FTC Act" means the Federal Trade Commission Act (15 U.S.C. 41 et seq.).

(8) HEADER INFORMATION.—The term "header information" means the source, destination, and routing information attached

to an electronic mail message, including the originating domain name and originating electronic mail address, and any other information that appears in the line identifying, or purporting to identify, a person initiating the message.

(9) INITIATE.—The term "initiate", when used with respect to a commercial electronic mail message, means to originate or transmit such message or to procure the origination or transmission of such message, but shall not include actions that constitute routine conveyance of such message. For purposes of this paragraph, more than one person may be considered to have initiated a message.

(10) INTERNET.—The term "Internet" has the meaning given that term in the Internet Tax Freedom Act (47 U.S.C. 151 nt).

(11) INTERNET ACCESS SERVICE.—The term "Internet access service" has the meaning given that term in section 231(e)(4) of the Communications Act of 1934 (47 U.S.C. 231(e)(4)).

(12) PROCURE.—The term "procure", when used with respect to the initiation of a commercial electronic mail message, means intentionally to pay or provide other consideration to, or induce, another person to initiate such a message on one's behalf.

(13) PROTECTED COMPUTER.—The term "protected computer" has the meaning given that term in section 1030(e)(2)(B) of title 18, United States Code.

(14) RECIPIENT.—The term "recipient", when used with respect to a commercial electronic mail message, means an authorized user of the electronic mail address to which the message was sent or delivered. If a recipient of a commercial electronic mail message has one or more electronic mail addresses in addition to the address to which the message was sent or delivered, the recipient shall be treated as a separate recipient with respect to each such address. If an electronic mail address is reassigned to a new user, the new user shall not be treated as a recipient of any commercial electronic mail message sent or delivered to that address before it was reassigned.

(15) ROUTINE CONVEYANCE.—The term "routine conveyance" means the transmission, routing, relaying, handling, or storing, through an automatic technical process, of an electronic mail

message for which another person has identified the recipients or provided the recipient addresses.

(16) SENDER.—

(A) IN GENERAL.—Except as provided in subparagraph (B), the term "sender", when used with respect to a commercial electronic mail message, means a person who initiates such a message and whose product, service, or Internet web site is advertised or promoted by the message.

(B) SEPARATE LINES OF BUSINESS OR DIVISIONS.—If an entity operates through separate lines of business or divisions and holds itself out to the recipient throughout the message as that particular line of business or division rather than as the entity of which such line of business or division is a part, then the line of business or the division shall be treated as the sender of such message for purposes of this Act.

(17) TRANSACTIONAL OR RELATIONSHIP MESSAGE.—

(A) IN GENERAL.—The term "transactional or relationship message" means an electronic mail message the primary purpose of which is—

(i) to facilitate, complete, or confirm a commercial transaction that the recipient has previously agreed to enter into with the sender;

(ii) to provide warranty information, product recall information, or safety or security information with respect to a commercial product or service used or purchased by the recipient;

(iii) to provide—

(I) notification concerning a change in the terms or features of;

(II) notification of a change in the recipient's standing or status with respect to; or

(III) at regular periodic intervals, account balance information or other type of account statement with respect to, a subscription, membership, account, loan, or comparable ongoing commercial relationship involving the ongoing purchase or use by the recipient of products or services offered by the sender;

(iv) to provide information directly related to an employment relationship or related benefit plan in which the recipient is currently involved, participating, or enrolled; or

(v) to deliver goods or services, including product updates or upgrades, that the recipient is entitled to receive under the terms of a transaction that the recipient has previously agreed to enter into with the sender.

(B) MODIFICATION OF DEFINITION.—The Commission by regulation pursuant to section 13 may modify the definition in subparagraph (A) to expand or contract the categories of messages that are treated as transactional or relationship messages for purposes of this Act to the extent that such modification is necessary to accommodate changes in electronic mail technology or practices and accomplish the purposes of this Act.

SEC. 4. PROHIBITION AGAINST PREDATORY AND ABUSIVE COMMERCIAL E-MAIL

(a) OFFENSE.—

(1) IN GENERAL.—Chapter 47 of title 18, United States Code, is amended by adding at the end the following new section:

"§1037. Fraud and related activity in connection with electronic mail

"(a) IN GENERAL.—Whoever, in or affecting interstate or foreign commerce, knowingly"

(1) accesses a protected computer without authorization, and intentionally initiates the transmission of multiple commercial electronic mail messages from or through such computer, "

(2) uses a protected computer to relay or retransmit multiple commercial electronic mail messages, with the intent to deceive or mislead recipients, or any Internet access service, as to the origin of such messages, "

(3) materially falsifies header information in multiple commercial electronic mail messages and intentionally initiates the transmission of such messages, "

(4) registers, using information that materially falsifies the identity of the actual registrant, for five or more electronic mail accounts or online user accounts or two or more domain names, and intentionally initiates the transmission of multiple commercial electronic mail messages from any combination of such accounts or domain names, or"

(5) falsely represents oneself to be the registrant or the legitimate successor in interest to the registrant of 5 or more Internet Protocol addresses, and intentionally initiates the transmission of multiple commercial electronic mail messages from such addresses, or conspires to do so, shall be punished as provided in subsection (b).

"(b) PENALTIES.—The punishment for an offense under subsection (a) is"

(1) a fine under this title, imprisonment for not more than 5 years, or both, if"

(A) the offense is committed in furtherance of any felony under the laws of the United States or of any State; or "

(B) the defendant has previously been convicted under this section or section 1030, or under the law of any State for conduct involving the transmission of multiple commercial electronic mail messages or unauthorized access to a computer system; "

(2) a fine under this title, imprisonment for not more than 3 years, or both, if"

(A) the offense is an offense under subsection (a)(1); "

(B) the offense is an offense under subsection (a)(4) and involved 20 or more falsified electronic mail or online user account registrations, or 10 or more falsified domain name registrations; "

(C) the volume of electronic mail messages transmitted in furtherance of the offense exceeded 2,500 during any 24-hour period, 25,000 during any 30-day period, or 250,000 during any 1-year period; "

(D) the offense caused loss to one or more persons aggregating $5,000 or more in value during any 1-year period; "

(E) as a result of the offense any individual committing the offense obtained anything of value aggregating $5,000 or more during any 1-year period; or "

(F) the offense was undertaken by the defendant in concert with three or more other persons with respect to whom the defendant occupied a position of organizer or leader; and "(3) a fine under this title or imprisonment for not more than 1 year, or both, in any other case.

"(c) FORFEITURE.—

"(1) IN GENERAL.—The court, in imposing sentence on a person who is convicted of an offense under this section, shall order that the defendant forfeit to the United States"

(A) any property, real or personal, constituting or traceable to gross proceeds obtained from such offense; and "

(B) any equipment, software, or other technology used or intended to be used to commit or to facilitate the commission of such offense.

"(2) PROCEDURES.—The procedures set forth in section 413 of the Controlled Substances Act (21 U.S.C. 853), other than subsection (d) of that section, and in Rule 32.2 of the Federal Rules of Criminal Procedure, shall apply to all stages of a criminal forfeiture proceeding under this section.

"(d) DEFINITIONS.—In this section:

"(1) LOSS.—The term 'loss' has the meaning given that term in section 1030(e) of this title.

"(2) MATERIALLY.—For purposes of paragraphs (3) and (4) of subsection (a), header information or registration information is materially falsified if it is altered or concealed in a manner that would impair the ability of a recipient of the message, an Internet access service processing the message on behalf of a recipient, a person alleging a violation of this section, or a law enforcement agency to identify, locate, or respond to a person who initiated the electronic mail message or to investigate the alleged violation.

"(3) MULTIPLE.—The term 'multiple' means more than 100 electronic mail messages during a 24-hour period, more than 1,000 electronic mail messages during a 30-day period, or more than 10,000 electronic mail messages during a 1-year period.

"(4) OTHER TERMS.—Any other term has the meaning given that term by section 3 of the CAN-SPAM Act of 2003.".

(2) CONFORMING AMENDMENT.—The chapter analysis for chapter 47 of title 18, United States Code, is amended by adding at the end the following:

"Sec.
"1037. Fraud and related activity in connection with electronic mail.".

(b) UNITED STATES SENTENCING COMMISSION.—

(1) DIRECTIVE.—Pursuant to its authority under section 994(p) of title 28, United States Code, and in accordance with this section, the United States Sentencing Commission shall review and, as appropriate, amend the

sentencing guidelines and policy statements to provide appropriate penalties for violations of section 1037 of title 18, United States Code, as added by this section, and other offenses that may be facilitated by the sending of large quantities of unsolicited electronic mail.

(2) REQUIREMENTS.—In carrying out this subsection, the Sentencing Commission shall consider providing sentencing enhancements for—

(A) those convicted under section 1037 of title 18, United States Code, who—

(i) obtained electronic mail addresses through improper means, including—

(I) harvesting electronic mail addresses of the users of a website, proprietary service, or other online public forum operated by another person, without the authorization of such person; and

(II) randomly generating electronic mail addresses by computer; or

(ii) knew that the commercial electronic mail messages involved in the offense contained or advertised an Internet domain for which the registrant of the domain had provided false registration information; and

(B) those convicted of other offenses, including offenses involving fraud, identity theft, obscenity, child pornography, and the sexual exploitation of children, if such offenses involved the sending of large quantities of electronic mail.

(c) SENSE OF CONGRESS.—It is the sense of Congress that—

(1) Spam has become the method of choice for those who distribute pornography, perpetrate fraudulent schemes, and introduce viruses, worms, and Trojan horses into personal and business computer systems; and

(2) the Department of Justice should use all existing law enforcement tools to investigate and prosecute those who send bulk commercial e-mail to facilitate the commission of Federal crimes, including the tools contained in chapters 47 and 63 of title 18, United States Code (relating to fraud and false statements); chapter 71 of title 18, United States Code (relating to obscenity); chapter 110 of title 18, United States Code (relating to the sexual exploitation of children); and chapter 95 of title 18, United States Code (relating to racketeering), as appropriate.

SEC. 5. OTHER PROTECTIONS FOR USERS OF COMMERCIAL ELECTRONIC MAIL

(a) REQUIREMENTS FOR TRANSMISSION OF MESSAGES.—

(1) PROHIBITION OF FALSE OR MISLEADING TRANSMISSION INFORMATION.—It is unlawful for any person to initiate the transmission, to a protected computer, of a commercial electronic mail message, or a transactional or relationship message, that contains, or is accompanied by, header information that is materially false or materially misleading. For purposes of this paragraph—

(A) header information that is technically accurate but includes an originating electronic mail address, domain name, or Internet Protocol address the access to which for purposes of initiating the message was obtained by means of false or fraudulent pretenses or representations shall be considered materially misleading;

(B) a "from" line (the line identifying or purporting to identify a person initiating the message) that accurately identifies any person who initiated the message shall not be considered materially false or materially misleading; and

(C) header information shall be considered materially misleading if it fails to identify accurately a protected computer used to initiate the message because the person initiating the message knowingly uses another protected computer to relay or retransmit the message for purposes of disguising its origin.

(2) PROHIBITION OF DECEPTIVE SUBJECT HEADINGS.—It is unlawful for any person to initiate the transmission to a protected computer of a commercial electronic mail message if such person has actual knowledge, or knowledge fairly implied on the basis of objective circumstances, that a subject heading of the message would be likely to mislead a recipient, acting reasonably under the circumstances, about a material fact regarding the contents or subject matter of the message (consistent with the criteria used in enforcement of section 5 of the Federal Trade Commission Act (15 U.S.C. 45)).

(3) INCLUSION OF RETURN ADDRESS OR COMPARABLE MECHANISM IN COMMERCIAL ELECTRONIC MAIL.—

(A) IN GENERAL.—It is unlawful for any person to initiate the transmission to a protected computer of a commercial electronic mail message that does not contain a functioning return electronic mail address or other Internet-based mechanism, clearly and conspicuously displayed, that—

(i) a recipient may use to submit, in a manner specified in the message, a reply electronic mail message or other form of Internet-based communication requesting not to receive future commercial electronic mail messages from that sender at the electronic mail address where the message was received; and

(ii) remains capable of receiving such messages or communications for no less than 30 days after the transmission of the original message.

(B) MORE DETAILED OPTIONS POSSIBLE.—The person initiating a commercial electronic mail message may comply with subparagraph (A)(i) by providing the recipient a list or menu from which the recipient may choose the specific types of commercial electronic mail messages the recipient wants to receive or does not want to receive from the sender, if the list or menu includes an option under which the recipient may choose not to receive any commercial electronic mail messages from the sender.

(C) TEMPORARY INABILITY TO RECEIVE MESSAGES OR PROCESS REQUESTS.—A return electronic mail address or other mechanism does not fail to satisfy the requirements of subparagraph (A) if it is unexpectedly and temporarily unable to receive messages or process requests due to a technical problem beyond the control of the sender if the problem is corrected within a reasonable time period.

(4) PROHIBITION OF TRANSMISSION OF COMMERCIAL ELECTRONIC MAIL AFTER OBJECTION.—

(A) IN GENERAL.—If a recipient makes a request using a mechanism provided pursuant to paragraph (3) not to receive some or any commercial electronic mail messages from such sender, then it is unlawful—

(i) for the sender to initiate the transmission to the recipient, more than 10 business days after the receipt of such request, of a commercial electronic mail message that falls within the scope of the request;

(ii) for any person acting on behalf of the sender to initiate the transmission to the recipient, more than 10 business days after the receipt of such request, of a commercial electronic mail message with actual knowledge, or knowledge fairly implied on the basis of objective circumstances, that such message falls within the scope of the request;

(iii) for any person acting on behalf of the sender to assist in initiating the transmission to the recipient, through the provision or selection of addresses to which the message will be sent, of a commercial electronic mail message with actual knowledge, or knowledge fairly implied on the basis of objective circumstances, that such message would violate clause (i) or (ii); or (iv) for the sender, or any other person who knows that the recipient has made such a request, to sell, lease, exchange, or otherwise transfer or release the electronic mail address of the recipient (including through any transaction or other transfer involving mailing lists bearing the electronic mail address of the recipient) for any purpose other than compliance with this Act or other provision of law.

(B) SUBSEQUENT AFFIRMATIVE CONSENT.—A prohibition in subparagraph (A) does not apply if there is affirmative consent by the recipient subsequent to the request under subparagraph (A).

(5) INCLUSION OF IDENTIFIER, OPT-OUT, AND PHYSICAL ADDRESS IN COMMERCIAL ELECTRONIC MAIL.—

(A) It is unlawful for any person to initiate the transmission of any commercial electronic mail message to a protected computer unless the message provides—

(i) clear and conspicuous identification that the message is an advertisement or solicitation;

(ii) clear and conspicuous notice of the opportunity under paragraph (3) to decline to receive further commercial electronic mail messages from the sender; and

(iii) a valid physical postal address of the sender.

(B) Subparagraph (A)(i) does not apply to the transmission of a commercial electronic mail message if the recipient has given prior affirmative consent to receipt of the message.

(6) MATERIALLY.—For purposes of paragraph (1), the term "materially", when used with respect to false or misleading header information, includes the alteration or concealment of header information in a manner that would impair the ability of an Internet access service processing the message on behalf of a recipient, a person alleging a violation of this section, or a law enforcement agency to identify, locate, or respond to a person who initiated the electronic mail message or to investigate the alleged violation, or the ability of a recipient of the message to respond to a person who initiated the electronic message.

(b) AGGRAVATED VIOLATIONS RELATING TO COMMERCIAL ELECTRONIC MAIL.—

(1) ADDRESS HARVESTING AND DICTIONARY ATTACKS.—

(A) IN GENERAL.—It is unlawful for any person to initiate the transmission, to a protected computer, of a commercial electronic mail message that is unlawful under subsection (a), or to assist in the origination of such message through the provision or selection of addresses to which the message will be transmitted, if such person had actual knowledge, or knowledge fairly implied on the basis of objective circumstances, that—

(i) the electronic mail address of the recipient was obtained using an automated means from an Internet website or proprietary online service operated by another person, and such website or online service included, at the time the address was obtained, a notice stating that the operator of such website or online service will not give, sell, or otherwise transfer addresses maintained by such website or online service to any other party for the purposes of initiating, or enabling others to initiate, electronic mail messages; or

(ii) the electronic mail address of the recipient was obtained using an automated means that gen- erates possible electronic mail addresses by combining names, letters, or numbers into numerous permutations.

(B) DISCLAIMER.—Nothing in this paragraph creates an ownership or proprietary interest in such electronic mail addresses.

(2) AUTOMATED CREATION OF MULTIPLE ELECTRONIC MAIL ACCOUNTS.—It is unlawful for any person to use scripts or other automated means to register for multiple electronic mail accounts or online user accounts from which to transmit to a protected computer, or enable another person to transmit to a protected computer, a commercial electronic mail message that is unlawful under subsection (a).

(3) RELAY OR RETRANSMISSION THROUGH UNAUTHORIZED ACCESS.—It is unlawful for any person knowingly to relay or retransmit a commercial electronic mail message that is unlawful under subsection (a) from a protected computer or computer network that such person has accessed without authorization.

(c) SUPPLEMENTARY RULEMAKING AUTHORITY.—The Commission shall by regulation, pursuant to section 13—

(1) modify the 10-business-day period under subsection (a)(4)(A) or subsection (a)(4)(B), or both, if the Commission determines that a different period would be more reasonable after taking into account—

(A) the purposes of subsection (a);

(B) the interests of recipients of commercial electronic mail; and

(C) the burdens imposed on senders of lawful commercial electronic mail; and

(2) specify additional activities or practices to which subsection (b) applies if the Commission determines that those activities or practices are contributing substantially to the proliferation of commercial electronic mail messages that are unlawful under subsection (a).

(d) REQUIREMENT TO PLACE WARNING LABELS ON COMMERCIAL ELECTRONIC MAIL CONTAINING SEXUALLY ORIENTED MATERIAL.—

(1) IN GENERAL.—No person may initiate in or affecting interstate commerce the transmission, to a protected computer, of any commercial electronic mail message that includes sexually oriented material and—

(A) fail to include in subject heading for the electronic mail message the marks or notices prescribed by the Commission under this subsection; or
(B) fail to provide that the matter in the message that is initially viewable to the recipient, when the message is opened by any recipient and absent any further actions by the recipient, includes only—

(i) to the extent required or authorized pursuant to paragraph (2), any such marks or notices;
(ii) the information required to be included in the message pursuant to subsection (a)(5); and
(iii) instructions on how to access, or a mechanism to access, the sexually oriented material.

(2) PRIOR AFFIRMATIVE CONSENT.—Paragraph (1) does not apply to the transmission of an electronic mail message if the recipient has given prior affirmative consent to receipt of the message.

(3) PRESCRIPTION OF MARKS AND NOTICES.—Not later than 120 days after the date of the enactment of this Act, the Commission in consultation with the Attorney General shall

prescribe clearly identifiable marks or notices to be included in or associated with commercial electronic mail that contains sexually oriented material, in order to inform the recipient of that fact and to facilitate filtering of such electronic mail. The Commission shall publish in the Federal Register and provide notice to the public of the marks or notices prescribed under this paragraph.

(4) DEFINITION.—In this subsection, the term "sexually oriented material" means any material that depicts sexually explicit conduct (as that term is defined in section 2256 of title 18, United States Code), unless the depiction constitutes a small and insignificant part of the whole, the remainder of which is not primarily devoted to sexual matters.

(5) PENALTY.—Whoever knowingly violates paragraph (1) shall be fined under title 18, United States Code, or imprisoned not more than 5 years, or both.

SEC. 6. BUSINESSES KNOWINGLY PROMOTED BY ELECTRONIC MAIL WITH FALSE OR MISLEADING TRANSMISSION INFORMATION

(a) IN GENERAL.—It is unlawful for a person to promote, or allow the promotion of, that person's trade or business, or goods, products, property, or services sold, offered for sale, leased or offered for lease, or otherwise made available through that trade or business, in a commercial electronic mail message the transmission of which is in violation of section 5(a)(1) if that person—

(1) knows, or should have known in the ordinary course of that person's trade or business, that the goods, products, property, or services sold, offered for sale, leased or offered for lease, or otherwise made available through that trade or business were being promoted in such a message;

(2) received or expected to receive an economic benefit from such promotion; and

(3) took no reasonable action—

(A) to prevent the transmission; or

(B) to detect the transmission and report it to the Commission.

(b) LIMITED ENFORCEMENT AGAINST THIRD PARTIES.—

(1) IN GENERAL.—Except as provided in paragraph (2), a person (hereinafter referred to as the "third party") that provides goods, products, property, or services to another person that violates subsection (a) shall not be held liable for such violation.

(2) EXCEPTION.—Liability for a violation of subsection (a) shall be imputed to a third party that provides goods, products, property, or services to another person that violates subsection (a) if that third party—

(A) owns, or has a greater than 50 percent ownership or economic interest in, the trade or business of the person that violated subsection (a); or

(B)(i) has actual knowledge that goods, products, property, or services are promoted in a commercial electronic mail message the transmission of which is in violation of section 5(a)(1); and

(ii) receives, or expects to receive, an economic benefit from such promotion.

(c) EXCLUSIVE ENFORCEMENT BY FTC.—Subsections (f) and (g) of section 7 do not apply to violations of this section.

(d) SAVINGS PROVISION.—Except as provided in section 7(f)(8), nothing in this section may be construed to limit or prevent any action that may be taken under this Act with respect to any violation of any other section of this Act.

SEC. 7. ENFORCEMENT GENERALLY

(a) VIOLATION IS UNFAIR OR DECEPTIVE ACT OR PRACTICE.—
Except as provided in subsection (b), this Act shall be enforced by
the Commission as if the violation of this Act were an unfair or
deceptive act or practice proscribed under section 18(a)(1)(B) of the
Federal Trade Commission Act (15 U.S.C. 57a(a)(1)(B)).

(b) ENFORCEMENT BY CERTAIN OTHER AGENCIES.—Compliance
with this Act shall be enforced—

(1) under section 8 of the Federal Deposit Insurance Act
(12 U.S.C. 1818), in the case of—

(A) national banks, and Federal branches and Federal
agencies of foreign banks, by the Office of the Comptroller
of the Currency;

(B) member banks of the Federal Reserve System
(other than national banks), branches and agencies of
foreign banks (other than Federal branches, Federal
agencies, and insured State branches of foreign banks),
commercial lending companies owned or controlled by
foreign banks, organizations operating under section 25 or
25A of the Federal Reserve Act (12 U.S.C. 601 and 611),
and bank holding companies, by the Board;

(C) banks insured by the Federal Deposit Insurance
Corporation (other than members of the Federal Reserve
System) and insured State branches of foreign banks, by
the Board of Directors of the Federal Deposit Insurance
Corporation; and

(D) savings associations the deposits of which are
insured by the Federal Deposit Insurance Corporation, by
the Director of the Office of Thrift Supervision;

(2) under the Federal Credit Union Act (12 U.S.C. 1751 et
seq.) by the Board of the National Credit Union
Administration with respect to any Federally insured credit
union;

(3) under the Securities Exchange Act of 1934 (15 U.S.C. 78a et seq.) by the Securities and Exchange Commission with respect to any broker or dealer;

(4) under the Investment Company Act of 1940 (15 U.S.C. 80a–1 et seq.) by the Securities and Exchange Commission with respect to investment companies;

(5) under the Investment Advisers Act of 1940 (15 U.S.C. 80b–1 et seq.) by the Securities and Exchange Commission with respect to investment advisers registered under that Act;

(6) under State insurance law in the case of any person engaged in providing insurance, by the applicable State insurance authority of the State in which the person is domiciled, subject to section 104 of the Gramm-Bliley-Leach Act (15 U.S.C. 6701), except that in any State in which the State insurance authority elects not to exercise this power, the enforcement authority pursuant to this Act shall be exercised by the Commission in accordance with subsection (a);

(7) under part A of subtitle VII of title 49, United States Code, by the Secretary of Transportation with respect to any air carrier or foreign air carrier subject to that part;

(8) under the Packers and Stockyards Act, 1921 (7 U.S.C. 181 et seq.) (except as provided in section 406 of that Act (7 U.S.C. 226, 227)), by the Secretary of Agriculture with respect to any activities subject to that Act;

(9) under the Farm Credit Act of 1971 (12 U.S.C. 2001 et seq.) by the Farm Credit Administration with respect to any Federal land bank, Federal land bank association, Federal intermediate credit bank, or production credit association; and

(10) under the Communications Act of 1934 (47 U.S.C. 151 et seq.) by the Federal Communications Commission with respect to any person subject to the provisions of that Act.

(c) EXERCISE OF CERTAIN POWERS.—For the purpose of the exercise by any agency referred to in subsection (b) of its powers under any Act referred to in that subsection, a violation of this Act is deemed to be a violation of a Federal Trade Commission trade regulation rule. In addition to its powers under any provision of law specifically referred to in subsection (b), each of the agencies referred to in that subsection may exercise, for the purpose of enforcing compliance with any requirement imposed under this Act, any other authority conferred on it by law.

(d) ACTIONS BY THE COMMISSION.—The Commission shall prevent any person from violating this Act in the same manner, by the same means, and with the same jurisdiction, powers, and duties as though all applicable terms and provisions of the Federal Trade Commission Act (15 U.S.C. 41 et seq.) were incorporated into and made a part of this Act. Any entity that violates any provision of that subtitle is subject to the penalties and entitled to the privileges and immunities provided in the Federal Trade Commission Act in the same manner, by the same means, and with the same jurisdiction, power, and duties as though all applicable terms and provisions of the Federal Trade Commission Act were incorporated into and made a part of that subtitle.

(e) AVAILABILITY OF CEASE-AND-DESIST ORDERS AND INJUNCTIVE RELIEF WITHOUT SHOWING OF KNOWLEDGE.—Notwithstanding any other provision of this Act, in any proceeding or action pursuant to subsection (a), (b), (c), or (d) of this section to enforce compliance, through an order to cease and desist or an injunction, with section 5(a)(1)(C), section 5(a)(2), clause (ii), (iii), or (iv) of section 5(a)(4)(A), section 5(b)(1)(A), or section 5(b)(3), neither the Commission nor the Federal Communications Commission shall be required to allege or prove the state of mind required by such section or subparagraph.

(f) ENFORCEMENT BY STATES.—

(1) CIVIL ACTION.—In any case in which the attorney general of a State, or an official or agency of a State, has reason to believe that an interest of the residents of that State has been or is threatened or adversely affected by any person who violates paragraph (1) or (2) of section 5(a), who violates section 5(d), or who engages in a pattern or practice that violates paragraph (3), (4), or (5) of section 5(a), of this Act, the attorney general, official, or agency of the State, as parens patriae, may bring a civil action on behalf of the residents of the State in a district court of the United States of appropriate jurisdiction—

exercising the powers conferred on the attorney general by the laws of that State to—

    (A) conduct investigations;
    (B) administer oaths or affirmations; or
    (C) compel the attendance of witnesses or the production of documentary and other evidence.

(7) VENUE; SERVICE OF PROCESS.—

    (A) VENUE.—Any action brought under paragraph (1) may be brought in the district court of the United States that meets applicable requirements relating to venue under section 1391 of title 28, United States Code.
    (B) SERVICE OF PROCESS.—In an action brought under paragraph (1), process may be served in any district in which the defendant—

        (i) is an inhabitant; or
        (ii) maintains a physical place of business.

(8) LIMITATION ON STATE ACTION WHILE FEDERAL ACTION IS PENDING.—If the Commission, or other appropriate Federal agency under subsection (b), has instituted a civil action or an administrative action for violation of this Act, no State attorney general, or official or agency of a State, may bring an action under this subsection during the pendency of that action against any defendant named in the complaint of the Commission or the other agency for any violation of this Act alleged in the complaint.

(9) REQUISITE SCIENTER FOR CERTAIN CIVIL ACTIONS.—Except as provided in section 5(a)(1)(C), section 5(a)(2), clause (ii), (iii), or (iv) of section 5(a)(4)(A), section 5(b)(1)(A), or section 5(b)(3), in a civil action brought by a State attorney general, or an official or agency of a State, to recover monetary damages for a violation of this Act, the court shall not grant the relief sought unless the attorney general, official, or agency establishes that the defendant acted with actual knowledge, or

knowledge fairly implied on the basis of objective
circumstances, of the act or omission that constitutes the
violation.

(g) ACTION BY PROVIDER OF INTERNET ACCESS SERVICE.—

(1) ACTION AUTHORIZED.—A provider of Internet access
service adversely affected by a violation of section 5(a)(1), 5(b),
or 5(d), or a pattern or practice that violates paragraph (2), (3),
(4), or (5) of section 5(a), may bring a civil action in any district
court of the United States with jurisdiction over the
defendant—

(A) to enjoin further violation by the defendant; or
(B) to recover damages in an amount equal to the
greater of—

(i) actual monetary loss incurred by the provider of
Internet access service as a result of such violation; or
(ii) the amount determined under paragraph (3).

(2) SPECIAL DEFINITION OF "PROCURE".—In any action
brought under paragraph (1), this Act shall be applied as if the
definition of the term "procure" in section 3(12) contained,
after "behalf" the words "with actual knowledge, or by
consciously avoiding knowing, whether such person is
engaging, or will engage, in a pattern or practice that violates
this Act".

(3) STATUTORY DAMAGES.—

(A) IN GENERAL.—For purposes of paragraph (1)(B)(ii),
the amount determined under this paragraph is the
amount calculated by multiplying the number of violations
(with each separately addressed unlawful message that is
transmitted or attempted to be transmitted over the
facilities of the provider of Internet access service, or that
is transmitted or attempted to be transmitted to an
electronic mail address obtained from the provider of

Internet access service in violation of section 5(b)(1)(A)(i), treated as a separate violation) by—

(i) up to $100, in the case of a violation of section 5(a)(1); or

(ii) up to $25, in the case of any other violation of section 5.

(B) LIMITATION.—For any violation of section 5 (other than section 5(a)(1)), the amount determined under subparagraph (A) may not exceed $1,000,000.

(C) AGGRAVATED DAMAGES.—The court may increase a damage award to an amount equal to not more than three times the amount otherwise available under this paragraph if—

(i) the court determines that the defendant committed the violation willfully and knowingly; or

(ii) the defendant's unlawful activity included one or more of the aggravated violations set forth in section 5(b).

(D) REDUCTION OF DAMAGES.—In assessing damages under subparagraph (A), the court may consider whether—

(i) the defendant has established and implemented, with due care, commercially reasonable practices and procedures designed to effectively prevent such violations; or

(ii) the violation occurred despite commercially reasonable efforts to maintain compliance with the practices and procedures to which reference is made in clause (i).

(4) ATTORNEY FEES.—In any action brought pursuant to paragraph (1), the court may, in its discretion, require an undertaking for the payment of the costs of such action, and assess

reasonable costs, including reasonable attorneys' fees, against any party.

SEC. 8. EFFECT ON OTHER LAWS

(a) FEDERAL LAW.—

(1) Nothing in this Act shall be construed to impair the enforcement of section 223 or 231 of the Communications Act of 1934 (47 U.S.C. 223 or 231, respectively), chapter 71 (relating to obscenity) or 110 (relating to sexual exploitation of children) of title 18, United States Code, or any other Federal criminal statute.

(2) Nothing in this Act shall be construed to affect in any way the Commission's authority to bring enforcement actions under FTC Act for materially false or deceptive representations or unfair practices in commercial electronic mail messages.

(b) STATE LAW.—

(1) IN GENERAL.—This Act supersedes any statute, regulation, or rule of a State or political subdivision of a State that expressly regulates the use of electronic mail to send commercial messages, except to the extent that any such statute, regulation, or rule prohibits falsity or deception in any portion of a commercial electronic mail message or information attached thereto.

(2) STATE LAW NOT SPECIFIC TO ELECTRONIC MAIL.—This Act shall not be construed to preempt the applicability of—

(A) State laws that are not specific to electronic mail, including State trespass, contract, or tort law; or
(B) other State laws to the extent that those laws relate to acts of fraud or computer crime.

(c) NO EFFECT ON POLICIES OF PROVIDERS OF INTERNET ACCESS SERVICE.—Nothing in this Act shall be construed to have any effect on the lawfulness or unlawfulness, under any other provision of law, of the adoption, implementation, or enforcement by a provider of Internet access service of a policy of declining to transmit, route, relay, handle, or store certain types of electronic mail messages.

SEC. 9. DO-NOT-E-MAIL REGISTRY

(a) IN GENERAL.—Not later than 6 months after the date of enactment of this Act, the Commission shall transmit to the Senate Committee on Commerce, Science, and Transportation and the House of Representatives Committee on Energy and Commerce a report that—

(1) sets forth a plan and timetable for establishing a nationwide marketing Do-Not-E-Mail registry;

(2) includes an explanation of any practical, technical, security, privacy, enforceability, or other concerns that the Commission has regarding such a registry; and

(3) includes an explanation of how the registry would be applied with respect to children with e-mail accounts.

(b) AUTHORIZATION TO IMPLEMENT.—The Commission may establish and implement the plan, but not earlier than 9 months after the date of enactment of this Act.

SEC. 10. STUDY OF EFFECTS OF COMMERCIAL ELECTRONIC MAIL

(a) IN GENERAL.—Not later than 24 months after the date of the enactment of this Act, the Commission, in consultation with the Department of Justice and other appropriate agencies, shall submit a report to the Congress that provides a detailed analysis of the effectiveness and enforcement of the provisions of this Act and the need (if any) for the Congress to modify such provisions.

(b) REQUIRED ANALYSIS.—The Commission shall include in the report required by subsection (a)—

(1) an analysis of the extent to which technological and marketplace developments, including changes in the nature of the devices through which consumers access their electronic mail messages, may affect the practicality and effectiveness of the provisions of this Act;

(2) analysis and recommendations concerning how to address commercial electronic mail that originates in or is transmitted through or to facilities or computers in other nations, including initiatives or policy positions that the Federal Government could pursue through international negotiations, fora, organizations, or institutions; and

(3) analysis and recommendations concerning options for protecting consumers, including children, from the receipt and viewing of commercial electronic mail that is obscene or pornographic.

SEC. 11. IMPROVING ENFORCEMENT BY PROVIDING REWARDS FOR INFORMATION ABOUT VIOLATIONS; LABELING

The Commission shall transmit to the Senate Committee on Commerce, Science, and Transportation and the House of Representatives Committee on Energy and Commerce—

(1) a report, within 9 months after the date of enactment of this Act, that sets forth a system for rewarding those who supply information about violations of this Act, including—

(A) procedures for the Commission to grant a reward of not less than 20 percent of the total civil penalty collected for a violation of this Act to the first person that—

(i) identifies the person in violation of this Act; and

(ii) supplies information that leads to the successful collection of a civil penalty by the Commission; and

(B) procedures to minimize the burden of submitting a complaint to the Commission concerning violations of this Act, including procedures to allow the electronic submission of complaints to the Commission; and

(2) a report, within 18 months after the date of enactment of this Act, that sets forth a plan for requiring commercial electronic mail to be identifiable from its subject line, by means of compliance with Internet Engineering Task Force Standards, the use of the characters ''ADV'' in the subject line, or other comparable identifier, or an explanation of any concerns the Commission has that cause the Commission to recommend against the plan.

SEC. 12. RESTRICTIONS ON OTHER TRANSMISSIONS

Section 227(b)(1) of the Communications Act of 1934 (47 U.S.C. 227(b)(1)) is amended, in the matter preceding subparagraph (A), by inserting '', or any person outside the United States if the recipient is within the United States'' after ''United States''.

SEC. 13. REGULATIONS

(a) IN GENERAL.—The Commission may issue regulations to implement the provisions of this Act (not including the amendments made by sections 4 and 12). Any such regulations shall be issued in accordance with section 553 of title 5, United States Code.

(b) LIMITATION.—Subsection (a) may not be construed to authorize the Commission to establish a requirement pursuant to section 5(a)(5)(A) to include any specific words, characters, marks, or labels in a commercial electronic mail message, or to include the identification required by section 5(a)(5)(A) in any particular part of such a mail message (such as the subject line or body).

SEC. 14. APPLICATION TO WIRELESS

(a) EFFECT ON OTHER LAW.—Nothing in this Act shall be
interpreted to preclude or override the applicability of section 227
of the Communications Act of 1934 (47 U.S.C. 227) or the rules
prescribed under section 3 of the Telemarketing and Consumer
Fraud and Abuse Prevention Act (15 U.S.C. 6102).

(b) FCC RULEMAKING.—The Federal Communications
Commission, in consultation with the Federal Trade Commission,
shall promulgate rules within 270 days to protect consumers from
unwanted mobile service commercial messages. The Federal
Communications Commission, in promulgating the rules, shall, to
the extent consistent with subsection (c)—

(1) provide subscribers to commercial mobile services the
ability to avoid receiving mobile service commercial messages
unless the subscriber has provided express prior authorization
to the sender, except as provided in paragraph (3);

(2) allow recipients of mobile service commercial messages
to indicate electronically a desire not to receive future mobile
service commercial messages from the sender;

(3) take into consideration, in determining whether to
subject providers of commercial mobile services to paragraph
(1), the relationship that exists between providers of such
services and their subscribers, but if the Commission
determines that such providers should not be subject to
paragraph (1), the rules shall require such providers, in
addition to complying with the other provisions of this Act, to
allow subscribers to indicate a desire not to receive future
mobile service commercial messages from the provider—

(A) at the time of subscribing to such service; and
(B) in any billing mechanism; and

(4) determine how a sender of mobile service commercial
messages may comply with the provisions of this Act,
considering the unique technical aspects, including the

functional and character limitations, of devices that receive such messages.

(c) OTHER FACTORS CONSIDERED.—The Federal Communications Commission shall consider the ability of a sender of a commercial electronic mail message to reasonably determine that the message is a mobile service commercial message.

(d) MOBILE SERVICE COMMERCIAL MESSAGE DEFINED.—In this section, the term "mobile service commercial message" means a commercial electronic mail message that is transmitted directly to a wireless device that is utilized by a subscriber of commercial mobile service (as such term is defined in section 332(d) of the Communications Act of 1934 (47 U.S.C. 332(d))) in connection with such service.

SEC. 15. SEPARABILITY

If any provision of this Act or the application thereof to any person or circumstance is held invalid, the remainder of this Act and the application of such provision to other persons or circumstances shall not be affected.

SEC. 16. EFFECTIVE DATE

The provisions of this Act, other than section 9, shall take effect on January 1, 2004.

Speaker of the House of Representatives.

Vice President of the United States and President of the Senate.

INDEX

A

access, 18, 19, 39, 41, 44, 45, 50, 60, 61, 62, 65, 66, 70, 72, 76, 77, 81, 82, 83, 88, 92, 95, 97, 99, 103, 105, 114, 117, 118
accuracy, 45, 60, 61
advertisements, 42, 58, 71, 72, 74
advertising, 2, 3, 16, 26, 32, 33, 39, 41, 42, 48, 62, 71, 73, 75, 76
affect, 36, 64, 116, 118
Albania, 29
ALI, 55
alternative, 19
amendments, 47, 53, 63, 81, 119
America Online, 15, 16, 17, 27
anti-spyware, 73, 76
Argentina, 29
association, 109
AT&T, 42, 46
attacks, 57, 67
attention, 59, 62
Attorney General, 7, 14, 105
Australia, 14, 29
Austria, 26
authentication, 2, 11, 19, 20, 21
authority, 36, 71, 73, 84, 91, 97, 109, 110, 116
availability, 48

B

backlash, 44
bad behavior, 75
banking, 78
bankruptcy, 62
banks, 35, 108
BBB, 20, 60
behavior, 20
Belgium, 26
Big Bang, 28
binding, 61
body, 12, 21, 119
Brazil, 25, 29
Britain, 26
browser, 66, 72
browsing, 71
Bulgaria, 29

C

California, 14, 15, 16, 34
calling party, 53
Canada, 25, 29
carrier, 45, 49, 50, 53, 55, 109
cell, 2, 14, 26, 39, 40, 42, 43, 44
cell phones, 2, 14, 26, 39, 43, 44
certificate, 20

J

K

L

M

time, 2, 6, 10, 11, 13, 20, 21, 32, 39, 42,
43, 44, 46, 48, 51, 55, 59, 60, 62, 66,
70, 71, 73, 75, 88, 90, 101, 103, 120
trade, 106, 107, 109
traffic, 1, 17, 31, 32, 88
transactions, 69, 78
transmission, 6, 8, 19, 32, 35, 36, 70, 73,
74, 80, 87, 92, 95, 99, 100, 101, 102,
103, 105, 106, 107
transmits, 57, 74
transparency, 71
transport, 21
trust, 46

U

uniform, 80
United Kingdom, 25, 29
United States, v, 4, 14, 35, 49, 87, 92,
94, 95, 96, 97, 98, 99, 106, 109, 110,
112, 113, 114, 116, 119, 121
universities, 18

V

validity, 11
variation, 20

Verizon, 42, 43, 44, 55
victims, 77, 83
viruses, 99
visual images, 12
voice, 40, 47

W

walking, 42
web, 61, 71, 93
web browser, 61
websites, 20, 25, 45, 46, 57, 58, 59, 60,
61, 62, 66, 67, 69, 84, 89
White House, 17, 65, 81
wireless devices, 2, 8, 14, 26, 40, 41, 42,
45, 48, 50
witnesses, 113
words, 18, 114, 119
work, 3, 10, 33, 48, 66
workplace, 77
worms, 99
worry, 10, 39, 41, 48
writing, 51, 53, 78

X

XML, 21